ROCKET CITY ROCK & SOUL

HUNTSVILLE MUSICIANS REMEMBER THE 1960s

JANE DENEEFE

Foreword by Frye Gaillard

THE History PRESS

Published by The History Press
Charleston, SC 29403
www.historypress.net

Cover design by Natasha Walsh

First published 2011

Manufactured in the United States

ISBN 978.1.60949.370.7

DeNeefe, Jane.
Rocket City rock and soul : Huntsville musicians remember the 1960s / Jane DeNeefe.
p. cm.
Includes bibliographical references and index.
ISBN 978-1-60949-370-7
1. Popular music--Alabama--Huntsville--1961-1970--History and criticism. I. Title.
ML3477.8.H86D46 2011
781.6409761'97--dc23
2011039235

Dedicated to my parents, Jane Kilbride and Bobby DeNeefe, who brought our young family to Huntsville in 1964 with their minds on our future.

Also dedicated to the memory of Adella Dale, who first told me about Huntsville's chitlin circuit twenty years before I understood that I should have recorded everything she said.

Contents

Foreword

The last time I worked with Jane DeNeefe, she was one of my coauthors on *Alabama's Civil Rights Trail: An Illustrated Guide to the Cradle of Freedom*. In addition to the chapters she wrote herself, she served as my guide to northern Alabama, and one of the stops we made together was the town of Muscle Shoals, where music had been a cornerstone of racial progress. Among other things, Muscle Shoals and the nearby towns of Sheffield, Tuscumbia and Florence had been home territory to W.C. Handy, "the Father of the Blues," and to Sam Phillips, who, among his many other musical distinctions, was the man who discovered Elvis Presley.

Presley and Phillips set out consciously to blend the black and white musical traditions of the South, and that same sensibility played out in the 1960s, when artists such as Arthur Alexander, Percy Sledge and Wilson Pickett began making records in Muscle Shoals. More often than not, these great African American artists cut their records with all-white studio bands, and these musicians—white and black—were proud of the fact that as racial tension ruled the day in other places, it was nonexistent in the recording studios of Muscle Shoals.

As Jane DeNeefe and I discussed such things, she said it reminded her of the musical traditions in her hometown of Huntsville, something I knew little about but found more and more fascinating as she talked. She told me of a friend named Ivy Joe Milan, who, in the 1960s, became lead singer for a racially integrated band called Ivy Joe and the Snowballs. A few months after that conversation, I had a chance to see Ivy Joe and his band in a reunion concert in Huntsville. It was a splendid display of rhythm and blues musicianship, and it was easy to imagine this particular band, in the 1960s, uniting the students in Huntsville's recently integrated high schools around their common love of soul music.

I remember mentioning to Jane that she should write about these Huntsville traditions and learning, in fact, that she had already begun. This book, the result of her years of extensive interviews, is more than a study of musical integration, as important as that subject may be. What DeNeefe understands and makes clear in these pages is that music often captures the spirit of the times, in all its various manifestations, and in that regard, the city of Huntsville was no exception. Among other things, Huntsville is home to Redstone Arsenal and thus played an integral role in the space race, particularly after 1957, when the Soviet Union launched its first Sputnik satellite.

The following year, when the United States launched its own Explorer satellite, with a rocket developed on the arsenal at Huntsville, the citizens of the town gathered in the streets to celebrate. A local band, Billy Hogan and the Twiliters, even wrote and recorded a song for the occasion, a rockabilly anthem that included these lines:

> *On a stormy night nineteen fifty eight*
> *Down in Rocket City history was made*
> *Well everybody went crazy, took to town*
> *Sirens wailing with a rockin' sound*

With a clear understanding of contemporary music—and the city in which she lives—Jane DeNeefe guides us through the Huntsville scene: the emerging funk artists, some of them still in high school, listening to the music of Thelonius Monk; the great blues singers like Howlin' Wolf playing the clubs in Huntsville's inner city; the rich and surprising contributions of Huntsville's 55th Army Band; and, of course, the beat of old-time rock 'n' roll. What DeNeefe has produced is a well-written case study of American music—how it shaped, and was shaped by, the life and history of one southern city. I never knew the full Huntsville story until now. I'm grateful to Jane for bringing it alive.

Frye Gaillard
Author, *Watermelon Wine: The Spirit of Country Music*

Preface

The Rocket City Rockophiles

Rocket City Rock and Soul grew out of a research project dubbed the Rocket City Rockophiles. The Rockophiles are a volunteer committee formed in 2005 to investigate rock and soul music in Huntsville. Librarian David Lilly, musician Jim Cavender, record collector Kip Shepherd and writer Jane DeNeefe form the core of the Rockophiles, though many others have assisted since our first interviews in 2005.

A rock and roll concert at the Huntsville–Madison County Public Library downtown was the genesis of the project, and the library's support has continued. In 2009, it sponsored the production of a compact disc called *Bookaroo*, featuring several of the musicians in this book, recorded live during a concert at the library.

You will get the most out of this book if you listen to music along with it. Every chapter mentions musicians, bands and songs that are worth finding. You can start with YouTube and Wikipedia or search real record stores. Facebook groups and fan websites are continuing to sprout.

Rocket City Rock and Soul is based on interviews with dozens of local musicians who played rock and soul in Huntsville in the 1960s. Some deserve whole books of their own. There is far more material than would fit here. Dozens of hours of interviews had to be transcribed, at first from analog tape and, later, from digital recordings. This daunting task required a small army of volunteers who were generous with their time and skills.

Help came in a variety of forms from many people, including Frye Gaillard, Penne Laubenthal, Jonathan Frazer, Jane and Kerry Kilbride,

Bobby and Donna DeNeefe, Lyndsey Torok, Pamela Watters, Doug Bennett, Ian McCalister, Stephen Waring, Rose Norman, William Hampton of Huntsville Revisited, Lance George of Huntsville Rewound, Caitilin Weber, Arianna Wolfe, David Person, Terri Cavender, Jana Savanapridi, Melissa Shepherd, Leigh Ann Coffield-Byrom, Rebecca Purcell, Michael David Smith, Thomas Hutchens, Sonnie Hereford IV, Thomas Hereford, Dede Gilbert Horan, Terry Cornett, Robert Burkhardt, Charlie Welch, Sophie Young, LeOtis Duvalier, the Daytons, John Shaver, Gloria Byrom Agrelius, Louise Jones McPhillips, Erin Reid, Rachel Dobson, Judy Watters, WLRH Sundial Writers' Corner, the *Huntsville Times*, the Valley Planet and Grant and Kathy Heath. Many thanks!

Photographs have been provided by musicians, their friends and families and by the archives department of the Huntsville–Madison County Public Library under the coordination of Susanna Leberman. The editors of The History Press have guided the book-creating process with the right balance of distance and availability.

Above all, *Rocket City Rock and Soul* would not have been possible without the musicians we consulted, listed here alphabetically: Terry Barkley, Bill Brandon, Billie Brown, James Butler, Larry Byrom, Adrian Clift, Chris Couchois, Mike Couchois, Pat Couchois, W.C. Cowles, Richard Crimes, Russell Crimes, Jedge Daniel, Randy Duck, Jimmy Gentry, Val Ginter, Mitch Glasgow, Tommy Graham, Danny Hall, Joe Hardin, Bucky Harris, Charlie Howell, Greg King, Butch Lacey, Charlie Langford, Stan Lee, Curtis Marshall, Howard Messer, Ivy Joe Milan, Bill Peck, Dan Pollock, Horace "Pap" Rice, Woody Richardson, Jack Robbins, Eddie Roberts, Ike Rooks, Tom Shepard, Toot Snoddy, Tim Spivey, George Vail, Dick Van Valkenberg, E.W. Wainright, Danny Warren, Vannie Warren, Ken Watters, Duke Way, Danny Wilder, Joe Williams, Tom Winstead Jr. and Tom Winstead Sr.

I have tried to present these musicians' stories with the highest respect for their opinions and life experiences. Any mistakes I may have made should not detract from the value of their contributions. *Rocket City Rock and Soul* is my thank-you gift for the hours of live music Huntsville's musicians have given me. I hope it inspires readers to listen more closely.

Introduction

From Cotton Market to Missile Command

Wherever people go, music goes, and Huntsville has been no exception. Huntsville had a fairly typical start for an Alabama town. Drawn by the presence of a very large spring, squatters lived in the area while it was still Chickasaw land. Once the government land sales started in 1809, wealthy planters bought large tracts that were quickly transformed into cotton plantations through the hard work of people of African descent who had been enslaved as a labor force. The town itself was laid out around our water source, the Big Spring. Huntsville's bounty of antebellum brick structures attests to the cotton wealth produced in Madison County in the nineteenth century.

By the early twentieth century, textile mills were moving into the area to process the cotton that was being grown. Rural citizens came to town to work in the mills. Dances were held in nearby Shelta Cave. By the beginning of World War II, Huntsville was very much like any other old southern town.

When the U.S. Army decided to base its Missile Command at Redstone Arsenal, Huntsville's transition to a city of the New South began. Through that same process, Huntsville's musical life was transformed.

In retrospect, two music pioneers with ties to Huntsville were bellwethers for the shift that was about to occur.

Above: Baptism at Big Spring. *Courtesy of Huntsville–Madison County Public Library.*

Below: Booley Monroe's Band. *Courtesy of Huntsville–Madison County Public Library.*

W.C. Handy, Father of the Blues

In the year 1900, William Hooper Councill, founder of Alabama A&M, hired W.C. Handy, who was not yet "Father of the Blues," to start a music program at the college. The problem with that, as Handy biographer David Robertson has pointed out, was that Councill "was no ragtime man." Councill's "understanding of music and his educational philosophy were in the utilitarian tradition of his fellow Alabama educator Booker T.

Washington." Councill "opposed the notion of a distinctive and independent African American musical aesthetic," preferring respectable European sounds, while complex, syncopated rhythms were holding Handy's attention. Handy was asked to leave his job in 1902 after he "affronted Councill by conducting a ragtime concert at a college assembly," but his influences have continued to reverberate throughout the world of music.

Sun Ra: "Space Is the Place"

In 1936, jazz innovator Sun Ra attended Alabama A&M, where he reportedly had a mystical experience that convinced him that he was really from Saturn. "Space is the place" became an important personal theme in his creative life. He once explained, "Any name I use other than Ra is a pseudonym." He was awarded a music scholarship at A&M under the "pseudonym" Herman Poole Blount.

Gifted at an early age, Ra was writing original songs by the time he was twelve. As a teenager, he could transcribe, from memory, big band performances he attended. His life experiences led him to observe, "The world has let down a lot of good musicians." In 1942, when Ra's conscientious objector status was rejected and he failed to report for service, he was arrested in Alabama for evading the draft.

Chapter 1

We're Standing on Their Shoulders

Origins of Huntsville Rock and Soul

Before he knew rock and roll, Larry Byrom wanted to play trumpet like Louis Armstrong. With a hairbrush for a microphone, Bill Brandon practiced in the mirror, singing doo-wop along with his Five Royals records. Adrian Clift, George Vail and Billie Brown all learned about harmony through shape note singing at church, while Curtis Marshall and his brothers seemed to absorb enough gospel and blues guitar from their family traditions to keep growing in step with the music of the times. Ivy Joe Milan was so nervous the first time he played a solo at marching band practice on the Councill High School football field that all he could manage was a four-count "bam bam bam bam," and the rest of the drum line broke up laughing.

Tom Shepard claims his first words were a whole sentence: "Get up and play that record." When Jedge Daniel heard Little Richard's "Tutti Frutti," all his previous music taste went "out the window." When he was still in elementary school, Mitch Glasgow would ride his stingray bike to the Couchoises' house and hang out in the driveway, listening to the teenage Couchois brothers practice. Huntsville's rock and roll community is rich with memories like these.

For some musicians, it was jazz that turned them on first. Val Ginter was lying in bed with the flu when Charlie Ventura and his Bop for the People entourage came on television, infusing him with the desire to hear more jazz. Richard Crimes appreciates Mr. Clarence Gandy, his teacher at Calvary Hill School, for making him sit down and listen to Thelonius Monk's

"Misterioso." His twin brother, Russell Crimes, remembers the time they had to decline going on the road with Howling Wolf and Arthur Conley because it would mean dropping out of high school. As a toddler, Greg King was drumming on the tables so much that his mother bought him a pair of bongos. Once Tommy Winstead tried bass, he lost interest in guitar.

Several of the people who played rock and soul music in Huntsville were first clued in to the secret language of scales and charts in their school bands, while others swapped chords with their friends and tried to imitate what they heard on records. At his family's music store, Jack Robbins "would just sit down and play with the instruments like it was a big toy store." The musicians we interviewed all remember the songs they heard on the radio. When they talk about the records they played over and over, they mean round black discs with paper labels in the center, played with real needles, on record players.

Drummer Horace Rice and trumpet player Butch Lacey both believe that popular music was able to flourish as it did in 1960s Huntsville because of the living legacy of previous generations of musicians. To Rice, musicians of his generation were "standing on the shoulders" of their teachers and mentors, older musicians whose roots reached back even further into history. Over generations, as Huntsville musicians have inspired one another, challenged one another, encouraged one another, jammed with one another and helped one another grow, the local music community has continued to evolve. Through concerts, records, radio and television, local musicians have drawn inspiration from great artists and from the cultural trends of the times. "We were all standing on somebody's shoulders," says Horace Rice, "but when you're young, you don't always know about the shoulders." The interview excerpts that follow show that when the musicians in this book reflect on their lives, they remember their early inspirations and influences.

Epiphanies

Bill Brandon realized too late that he had missed a chance to learn some authentic blues guitar techniques from his father. As a teenager, Brandon learned to tune the guitar in open E, which he called "E natural," and told his father it was the "new way," not realizing the value of the "old way" his father could have taught him:

> *My dad played some guitar and sang. He used to have a group, he and some friends who came over and played stuff I've never heard of*

before or since in my life. I can only remember some of the lyrics. He would pick old blues songs with lyrics like "If blues was whiskey" or "Throw your clothes out the window, let the shack burn down," you know, stuff like that. I'd fiddle around with the guitar and try to pick up the tune he was playing. Now I wish I'd learned more; he did try to teach me but I was thickheaded, a typical kid. I played in E natural. That's the way I started playing, and he couldn't understand that for nothing in the world. And me, Mr. Know-It-All, said, "Dad, this is the new way of tuning" and didn't learn how to make that sound he could make. Years later, I got with a friend of mine from Birmingham, Curtis Marshall. He was probably one of the best blues guitarists—if you listened to him with your eyes closed, you'd probably think it was B.B. King. He finally showed me how to tune the guitar the old way, and I went from there.

I was busy ripping and running, and nothing meant nothing but music. I used to go to the store and buy records, then listen to groups like the Coasters and the Five Royals on my old phonograph, standing in front of the mirror and holding a brush as a microphone, pretending to be onstage.

Tommy Graham's mother was a professional musician:

My mom played piano with the Tommy Dorsey Band. When she got pregnant with me, that took her out of the music business. But later she would play some gigs. She had taught me to play boogie-woogie where you rock your hand back and forth. Instead of the count going one-two-three-four-five-six-seven-eight, it would go "and one and two and three and four and five and six and seven eight," like that.

In 1957, the Ink Spots played in Nashville. My mother took me with her to meet and hear the band. In the afternoon before rehearsal, my mom and I did a piano routine together. The Spots heard it and asked me to come up and play it during the show. I would do the left-hand boogie-woogie part while she played the top end. I can remember that there were hundreds of people in the crowd, and I was scared shitless. That was the first time I was to play in front of an audience. They called me up and followed me with the spotlight. We played the number, and the crowd thundered with applause. I was smiling from ear to ear when I took my little bow and scurried off the stage. That was a defining moment in my life. That was the moment I knew I was going to play music as a career.

Joe Hardin's family had moved to Huntsville in 1949, before he was born, but their roots were in Birmingham:

> *I came from a musical family. My father had played piano in a band in Birmingham before World War II (they played in Tuxedo Junction, which was a real place in Birmingham). We all took piano lessons in Huntsville (Ms. Allen) because that was part of a "good" upbringing. My father had a great 78 collection with some Freddie Slack and Louis Jordan and Nat King Cole, so I grew up listening to the roots of rock and roll.*
>
> *My uncle was stationed on the base at the arsenal in the late '50s and had a huge Buddy Holly collection. He would come home from work every night and put "Peggy Sue" on the record player. Then he would take the arm off the record so it would repeat. He usually got about five repeats in before my dad would make him stop. So I grew up with Buddy Holly, Louis Jordan, Hoagy Carmichael and Nat King Cole.*

Larry Byrom may be best known around Huntsville as our local connection to Steppenwolf, but he started out loving Dixieland jazz:

> *I got into music because of Louis Armstrong. I wanted to be a trumpet player, so I started trumpet lessons at the age of seven and kept those lessons up 'til I was about fourteen. My teacher was very insightful, he taught me piano and how to read piano music along with the trumpet, because he said it was important to be able to know what you were playing, and if you could see it, you could relate to it better. So I got that instruction along the way until I got seriously involved with the Beatles, and the guitar just seemed fascinating to me. I'd always liked Chet Atkins and Merle Travis and a bunch of these guys who played a finger-picking style where you could accompany yourself. I was listening to Chet Atkins and copying his records and learning to play "Yankee Doodle" and "Dixie" at the same time. That was a big deal. Now, on trumpet you could just play one note at a time. Obviously, on piano you could play a stride and accompany yourself that way. But it was fascinating that with just six strings you could make so much more music, and that was the way I wanted to go.*
>
> *My brother Mike and I made a record when I was twelve years old and he was nine. It's two songs that I wrote, actually an old 45 that I still have, on the old Lawson label out of South Bend, Indiana, "Satisfaction" and "Contentment." I was a mellow person. "Contentment" was a ballad, and I played piano. Mike played a tenor saxophone just about as big as he was. I played trumpet. They were instrumentals, no lyrics.*

Above: Mike Byrom on saxophone, Larry Byrom on trumpet. *Courtesy of Larry Byrom.*

Left: Young Ivy Joe Milan. *Courtesy of Ivy Joe Milan.*

Horace Rice developed his love of drumming as a student at Councill High School:

> *I loved learning to play in different time signatures. Marching band is always in 4/4 time. At Councill High School, I had lessons from the band director, Edwin Hill, and one summer I studied with a drummer named*

Sox Smith at his drums, Alma Haygood on piano.
Courtesy of Thomas Hutchens.

Joe Ford, who played in combos and big bands, including a big band called Sox Smith. I don't know Smith's real name, but it was the Sox Smith Band. He told me how to play in 5/4, 3/4, 6/8, 9/8 times. I was a young man and I only played in 4/4 until I started studying with him, so he would show me how to play in those different time signatures. Telling me how to play in these different time signatures expanded my horizons, because when I was listening to some of the things that Basie and Duke were doing, there were times when I could count out one two three, one two three, but I hadn't played it and then—so now I'm thinking in other time signatures other than just 1-2-3-4, 2-2-3-4...so Joe Ford, I remember him for that. Because most of the marching band music is all in 4/4.

Bill Brandon also had Mr. Hill for a music teacher:

For junior high, I went to Calvary Hill. I started playing trumpet and got in the band. Mr. Edwin Hill was my teacher. I was pretty good with the thing. Sometimes Mr. Hill would step out of the practice room and say to me, "Bill, you're in charge; you keep everything going." When he'd come back, I'd have them rockin' to "Who Wears Short Shorts?" or something like that. He'd say, "Jesus! Please! Play the marching tune!"

I guess the rock and roll stuff started when I was at Winston Street School. I remember we were doing some kind of talent show in the lunchroom, which

> *served as our auditorium. I was doing an Elvis Presley bit, had painted on some sideburns and had on a pair of blue suede shoes I had gotten from somewhere. I had a guitar with no strings on it and was just pantomiming, and the girls would scream when I did the Elvis thing with my leg. I think I was doing "Don't Be Cruel." Oh yeah, all the girls screaming and stuff was real fine.*

Brandon points out that Elvis was popular with black kids at that time, explaining, "We knew what it was. We knew he was white and sounding black, but it was good and we liked it. We also listened to groups like the Five Royals, the Coasters, Ike and Tina and Jimmy Reed."

Brandon's younger cousin Ivy Joe Milan grew up near the intersection of Church at Holmes, in a house his family rented from Reverend Joseph Lowery's father. Ivy Joe's mother would wake them up in the morning with the record player blaring rock and roll:

> *I'd wake up every morning, you know, with my mom playing the Chuck Berry song, "up in the morning and off to school..." Then she'd say, "OK, let's roll."*
>
> *Musically, those were some great times. I had a lot of influences. I have to say that Elvis was an early influence. One time they had a talent show and I got up and did "Jail House Rock" because I had just seen the movie and I wiggled my leg like Elvis. The instructor told me to sit down and that I was nothing but a thug and was going to end up in jail; you know, she was right. In the fourth grade, I got called out of class a lot and told to go to the band room for punishment. I think I was beating on my desk like a set of bongos, and the teacher would throw me out and send me to the band room. Well, I'm still beating on them today!*
>
> *I listened to almost anything, even some country music on WBHP. I really liked Martha Reeves and the Vandellas, stuff like "Nowhere to Run" and "Dancing in the Streets." Oh yeah, I liked the Shirelles too, who did a song called "Boys." Actually, my favorite Shirelles song was called "Untie Me," which I performed later.*

Adrian Clift's childhood was full of music: gospel at church, band at school and a record player at home with country and rock and roll records.

> *I didn't realize it at the time, but Mother was quite a rocker for her age. I can't remember all the stuff she did have, but just a few of the records I probably wouldn't have bought as a six-year-old but listened to all the*

> *time were: "Blueberry Hill" by Fats Domino, "Hound Dog," "Don't Be Cruel" and "Blue Suede Shoes" by Elvis, "Bony Maroni" and "Long Tall Sally" (Little Richard). I wore those old 45 RPMs out. The next musical memory I have was of my Mother singing "Que Sera, Sera" right after we moved to Huntsville.*

Rhythm and blues guitarist Curtis Marshall was born outside of Birmingham on "the seventeenth day of the third month of 1943," the oldest of seven boys and one girl. He moved to Huntsville in 1963. Marshall did not study guitar formally but learned from his mother and his grandfather. One of his cousins, Luther Ingram, coauthored the Staple Singers' hit anthem "Respect Yourself."

> *First time I heard a guitar my grandfather was playing it. Such beautiful, melodious music came out of that guitar. Guitar has always inspired me and my brother. I didn't learn nothin' else but that damn guitar. That's all I could think about. I could sleep it, taste it.*
>
> *My grandfather James Haley played guitar fluently. He had a big guitar I couldn't get my arms around, and he kept that thing in a cedar cabinet. He came out of Waycross, Georgia. His people were musicians from the time of slavery on up. His ancestors entertained Jesse James. My grandfather could read formal sheet music, and I guess it rubbed off on me some kind of way. He would call out to me and my brother Burley, "Come on!" From then on, I started learning to play. He played blues like "Yella Gal": "When my baby left me, my mule laid down and died."*

Charlie Langford, who played a National guitar, explains, "They needed those songs like 'Yella Gal' back in the slave times, because they were under so much pressure." Curtis Marshall could practice on his grandfather's guitar at home, but he needed one of his own:

> *See, things were tight because we lived in the coal-mining district, all my people were coal miners and farmers, and if you lost your father, things were tight. Well, some old men heard I could play guitar. I was about twelve or so. And man, my first professional job was in Birmingham in Ensley, Alabama, at a club called the Downbeat. Oh lord, I was a child. They would let me play as long as I could and they'd put me to sleep under a table and then wake me up again, and it went on and on. They carried me home and paid me fifteen dollars. Every Friday they'd come and get me.*

So I went back in the woodshed and practiced and practiced and practiced. I worked cutting grass around people's houses and saw a guitar for sale. This old man had a Gibson for sale for thirteen dollars. "Mr. Wade, you still wanna sell that guitar? I got eight dollars." He said, "Boy, you're pretty honest. When can you bring me the rest?" I said, "I'll bring it next Friday when I get paid." So I did that. Put it in the closet with my grandfather's guitar, practiced that thing all night long.

Got some money together and went down to E.E. Forbes Music Company and got me an electronic pickup installed on it, converted it to an electric guitar, and an amplifier about as big as that beer can. I'm serious. It sounded about like a mouse in an outside toilet. My little amp was about as loud as a mosquito tweeter. I'm telling the truth. Ain't no use in procrastinatin' about it. At our high school talent show, the Marshall Brothers couldn't be beat.

Crossing Over

Music was changing along with society. Rhythm and blues, bluegrass music, rockabilly and rock and roll were emerging as new twists on older musical forms. Innovators like Sister Rosetta Tharp and Ray Charles blended rhythm and blues with a gospel feeling, a combination that people connected with instinctively and began to call "soul." Chuck Berry, Bill Haley, Bo Diddley and many others were plugging in instruments and emphasizing rock and roll beats. The same song might be sung by different artists and repackaged for different markets. After New York songwriters Lieber and Stoller wrote "Hound Dog" for Big Mama Thornton to record in 1952, several country bands recorded versions on small labels before Elvis took it all the way to the white mainstream.

With his prolific reinterpretations of other people's songs, Elvis epitomized the practice of borrowing from the creative accomplishments of previous artists. His renditions of old blues songs, country songs, show tunes and sacred music showed that all genres were fair game. Elvis's "Blue Moon of Kentucky" reached a wider audience than the Bill Monroe original.

Sometime in the late fifties, Jack Robbins had a small-town brush with a young Elvis Presley: "Of course, Elvis Presley was an icon at that time. I was from Tupelo, so we would go over there and he'd play the state fair. We had an opportunity to see him up close and meet the guy. It wasn't like we sat around and had a conversation. His family was from there. My cousins were friends with Elvis's cousins."

Larry Byrom wasn't into country music, but he remembers being attuned to rock sounds that had some twang:

> *In the sixties, there was an individual named Wayne Bridge, and I was fascinated with his guitar playing.*
>
> *Before that, there were three brothers called the Mitchell Brothers. Before the Peppermint was on the Parkway it was on Orchard, and we lived on Orchard. Price Mitchell was the lead singer, and he actually had a couple of releases in Nashville. They were kinda country. Country rock is what I would call it.*

Rock and Roll, Rhythm and Soul

Terry Barkley describes rock and roll:

> *To me, it's a combination of rockabilly, blues, country and R&B, a little bit of everything. You go back to early performers like Jerry Lee Lewis, certainly Little Richard and, of course, Elvis, you'll see they were drawing on a lot of musical influences. As a drummer, it was exciting to me that you now have a drummer playing an important role. In early rockabilly you've got a stand-up base with a guitar keeping the rhythm, but all of a sudden, you've got a drummer banging away during the performance. Buddy Holly and, eventually, Elvis had drummers, so you get a syncopated 4/4 beat driving the song. You know like on the* Dick Clark Show *where they would always say, "It's got a good beat that you can dance to. I'll give it an 8."*

"It was definitely about the beat," said Greg King, "and I'm not just saying that because I'm a drummer. Guitar is the icing on the cake, the flavor of it." Horace Rice explains the gradual influence of African American rhythms on mainstream culture:

> *In the fifties, a lot of younger whites were not being influenced by black music, but there was such a process of cross-pollination that by the end of the sixties, musical styles became less identifiable according to race. White musicians have told me that in the fifties they had to sneak to listen to black music. They wouldn't tell their parents.*
>
> *I didn't buy a lot of Elvis music. But Bill Haley, now, we liked some of the things that he did, because it was hard-driving rockabilly and it*

was good, you know, it had some degree of funk. It was a little different from rhythm and blues in terms of how the drummers and the bass players played, but you know it was good, you know musicianship was there. In a blues rhythm pattern, the emphasis was on the two and the four, with a little hesitation that has a funk feel. In a "white" rhythm pattern, the hesitation isn't there, or the emphasis might be on the one and the three. When I say it's a white beat, it's not bad, it's just different. The white beat was not soulful. That two and four, with a little hesitation, came out of New Orleans. They used to call it the New Orleans beat when drummers played it, and it sounded just like the second line dance today. It was distinctly New Orleans, and you borrowed, and inculcated, that two and four. I heard it in the Caribbean. And when I went to Senegal, same thing.

By the late sixties, you had the Allman Brothers, who were a white group who played funk. In the Allman Brothers you hear the two-four accents along the rhythm line. If you go back and listen to "I Want to Hold Your Hand," that's played in a white style. It rocks, but it isn't funky. But by the end of the sixties, almost complete cross-pollination.

Terry Barkley remembers the local drummers he admired when he was with the Shandells:

Locally, the best drummers I remember from the sixties were Jerry Brewer from the Tiks and the late, great Ray Sanderson of the Hi-Boys. Ray passed away. He was a wonderful guy and terrific drummer. He went to

Dino Danelli at the Coliseum.
Courtesy of Dede Gilbert Horan.

Ray Sanderson of the Hi Boys. *Courtesy of Terry Barkley.*

> *Butler a few years ahead of me. The Shandells probably learned more from the Hi-Boys than the Tiks; they were Butler people, and we knew them pretty well. Jerry could really kick it on the Tiks version of "Please, Please, Please." Laying down a steady and loud beat, driving the song, that's what they could do so well.*
>
> *Simple, driving rhythms with volume, that sums up good rock drumming to me, not drum solos. I admired Ringo and Charlie Watts of the Stones. They weren't flashy either, but they were solid. On the other hand, I remember seeing Dino Danelli of the Young Rascals play at the Coliseum. He was solid but also a great showman, twirling the sticks, the whole routine, but laying down a great beat. He just floored the audience.*

In *Blues for the White Boy*, guitarist Dan Pollock describes Ted Walton, who played drums for Sonny Davis and the Mastersound:

> *Ted was probably the best blues shuffle drummer that I ever played with. He was what we call, "in the pocket" and most importantly, he knew what not to play. A lot of drummers will take blues gigs because they need the money but really aren't in to the music itself and with that attitude they start adding things to the mix that don't belong. They get bored with it after a few tunes and they start to emulate Buddy Rich or Louis Bellson or somebody. For a drummer that's not into the blues and doesn't have it in his heart is going to have a very long night on a gig. A real blues drummer loves the music and takes in the overall picture*

and is always that steady back bone supporting the singers and soloists, constantly keeping the groove of the song going. A drummer cannot overplay in blues and has to keep it "in the pocket" for it to be right. At least, that's the way it was done where I came from. That's why I loved playing with Ted so much because he was the epitome of what a blues drummer is all about. He could kick ass on Memphis Soul too and he always pulled something extra out of me! Don't get me wrong, E.W. Wainwright is a monster drummer, still is and I loved playing with Wain and learning from him, but I still wanted that "Alabama Shuffle" and Wain just couldn't play it like Ted.

Val Ginter's time in Huntsville exposed him to local southern rhythms and styles:

The feeling is so personal. Pap Rice demonstrated soul drumming to me. And when combined with a Fender electric bass, it was a tremendous experience. I used to hear that music at the black American Legion in Huntsville and the black Elks. Joe Williams was a friend of Joe Tex, and he took me to the black American Legion one night to hear and meet Joe Tex. There was really a lot going on here.

They usually say that the first rock and roll record was "Sha Boom?" Mike Stoller and Jerry Lieber out of New York were writing things for Big Joe Turner and Big Mama Thornton. But the white stations wouldn't play those things because advertisers would cancel. So those tunes were all covered by white groups. I think "Shake, Rattle and Roll" was written for Turner, and it was covered by Bill Haley, and "You Ain't Nothing but a Hound Dog" was written for Thornton. And that was covered by Presley. And Little Richard dropped out to become a minister, studying at Oakwood College in Huntsville. So the music world went from race music to rhythm and blues to rock and roll (after rhythm and blues was mixed with country and western in order to appear on white radio stations).

Rather than think of soul music as an era or a genre, Bill Brandon takes a philosophical view of the relationship between rock and roll, blues and soul:

Rock and roll and soul? When you say soul, in my opinion that's what the individual puts into what he or she does. Soul has no color. Its origin is from within the individual. When you talk about rock and roll and blues, you're talking about different levels. When you say rock and roll, what comes in my mind is Little Richard, Eric Clapton, Tina Turner, and when you talk about blues, I think of the origin of blues.

Everyone's got soul that's got talent. You can write stuff, and read music, and I don't care how smart you are, it's how you interpret what you read, that's where soul comes in. What comes out of the bell of that horn—that's soul.

Chapter 2

Shake It Over Sputnik

Huntsville in the Fifties

Space Race

Right up until World War II, Huntsville's cultural trajectory was similar to that of any other mid-sized southern town. The close of World War II brought, for mainstream Americans, a busy period of patriotic fervor, consumerism and domesticity. Huntsville was not only involved in key changes taking place on the national scene, but it also contributed uniquely to a new national priority: the space race. After the war, key decisions at the federal level shifted Huntsville's course away from the priorities of the past. Locally, the economic transition from Old South to New South was propelled by missile technology.

In 1941, agricultural land near the Tennessee River was turned into Huntsville Arsenal, a facility in danger of being shut down by 1949. Instead of closing, the arsenal expanded when the U.S. Army based its rocket and missile operations there and changed the name to Redstone. In 1950, Werner Von Braun's team of German rocket scientists, more or less our nation's guests at Fort Bliss in Texas, were relocated to do their work at Redstone Arsenal, taking their oaths of U.S. citizenship at Huntsville High School in 1955. On October 4, 1957, when the Soviet Union succeeded in placing the first satellite, Sputnik, into Earth's orbit, Redstone's rocket scientists picked up their pace, launching the United States' first satellite, Explorer I, on January 31, 1958. By 1960, when NASA (National Aeronautics and Space Administration) was formed, the old cotton market town had become the rocket city.

Left: Army missile, antebellum bank. *Courtesy of Lance George, Huntsville Rewound.*

Below: Party guest Ed Laughlin plays Sox Smith's drums. Alma Haygood on piano, Ike Rooks far right, leaning forward. *Courtesy of Thomas Hutchens.*

Dancers at the Hutchens party, James Jamar on saxophone. *Courtesy of Thomas Hutchens.*

Historian David Halberstam devotes a chapter of his book *The Fifties* to Huntsville's role in the space program. To Halberstam, the space race began in Germany at the end of World War II when Stalin's troops got to the German rocket camp to find that the prize they sought was no longer there. Halberstam quotes Stalin as fuming, "We defeated Nazi armies, but the Americans got the rocket engineers." Winston Churchill considered the space race between the Russians and the Americans a "wizard war," but Halberstam explains, "Von Braun's knowledge was so complete and he easily blended the practical with the visionary." Colonel John Keck predicted, "This will make Buck Rogers look like he lived in the Gay Nineties."

Von Braun would need an army of engineers, technicians and other support personnel to make the vision a reality. Word went out, and kept going out, that Huntsville had jobs, especially for engineers. There were also jobs for carpenters, cashiers and cooks, as well as opportunities for businesses like restaurants, clothing stores, vending machines, radio stations, barbershops, nightclubs—anything a growing town could need.

Boomtown

Business in Huntsville boomed as military people and defense workers moved in. Many brought their families or started families after they got here. Their children formed the core of Huntsville's baby boom generation. There wasn't enough housing to accommodate them all, so a house-building boom ensued. Cotton fields, cow pastures, woods and meadows gave way to subdivision after subdivision with names like Blossomwood, Holiday Homes, Thornton Acres, Lakewood, Davis Hills and Mayfair.

The arsenal-stimulated growth of the early fifties had an ongoing ripple effect. In 1955, Jackson Berlin Robbins Sr. was teaching music at Itawamba Junior College in Mississippi and playing string bass for jazz trumpeter Al Hirt, with whom he had served in the army. Seeing Huntsville's business potential, he decided to move his young family here and open a music store downtown to sell band instruments. As a bassist, he joined the brand-new Huntsville Symphony Orchestra.

Adrian Clift was approaching first grade when his family arrived from middle Tennessee, so he had some basis for comparison:

> *I was born a baby boomer in a small town in middle Tennessee. The workers at the stove foundry where my father worked in the mid-fifties were on strike at the time; but in any case, he had heard about opportunities at the Army Ballistic Missile Agency in Huntsville, and he wound up landing a job there in early 1956. It probably did not hurt his cause that he had been a navy instructor in aircraft mechanics during the war and had afterward picked up a great deal of experience as a sheet metal craftsman. My dad commuted for maybe six months or so, eventually sharing a ride with a fellow from Fayetteville, before we moved to Huntsville in the summer of 1956. While my parents oversaw building of their new home on some property they had purchased on Mastin Lake Road, we rented a house a couple blocks from Terry Heights Elementary, where I started first grade that year.*
>
> *Cotton fields? Everywhere you looked. My uncle "Radio" would always give my dad a hard time about that "Alabama red dirt," but it was in a cotton field at Mastin Lake and the Parkway where I found my first Indian artifact. I have a love of southeastern Indian archaeology that continues to this day. North Alabama is a treasure-trove of archaeological sites.*

After NASA was established in 1960, the name became such a household word locally that in casual conversation it is also used to describe space-related work prior to 1960. Former Huntsvillian Frank Webb describes living in a neighborhood full of space workers:

> *In fact, I was about the only third-generation Huntsvillian that I knew. All four grandparents were from here. I was actually born in Knoxville (1953),*

where Dad was working for TVA at the time, but we moved back here when I was six months old, as NASA started to gear up. Virtually everyone I knew in Lakewood, where I grew up, were NASA folks from somewhere else. On any random day in Lakewood I could go visit someone and see a world-class musician playing the piano, or watch someone painting, or hear discourse on pre-Columbian Alabama history. You almost took it for granted beyond a certain point, just part of the landscape, like the roar of the rockets out on Redstone.

Rockabilly Days of the Late Fifties

Aspects of the Old South were also giving way to the new in the world of southern music. The mobility of the growing automotive culture and technological advances in amplification, recording techniques and broadcasting all drove musical innovation by increasing people's access to different kinds of songs and sounds. The music emerging wasn't entirely new, but it seemed to blend together various old genres and attitudes into unexpected flavors that were sometimes startling, even challenging. Something about the rhythms in the new music made people rock, and some of it was known as rockabilly.

According to Billy Joe Cooley, Grady Reeves lost money but was ahead of his time back in 1954 when he took a chance on booking some traveling musicians who needed work for the night. In Cooley's *Old Huntsville Magazine* story "Grady Reeves, the Promoter," he describes the arrival of a Cadillac limousine with a dozen people. "A rack on top of the car contained suitcases, guitars and amplifiers," Cooley writes. "It looked like a band of gypsies. The car was old, half covered with mud, and resembled something that had traveled across a lot of plowed fields in recent days." At the Madison County Coliseum, which "in those days had no end walls, since it was primarily used for cattle shows and such," a sparse local audience was blessed with a live show by Sun Studio road musicians who would become legends later: Carl Perkins, Johnny Cash, Jerry Lee Lewis and Elvis Presley.

Cooley doesn't tell us what songs they played that night, but Elvis's 1954 recordings are likely to have been in the mix. His cover of Arthur "Big Boy" Crudup's 1947 RCA Victor song "That's All Right Mama" would have been a possibility, as would its flip side, a rockabilly interpretation of Bill Monroe's "Blue Moon of Kentucky."

Above: Madison County Coliseum in the 1950s. *Courtesy of Huntsville–Madison County Public Library.*

Below: Aerial view of Madison County Coliseum, early 1960s. *Lower right*: intersection of Holmes Avenue and Highway 72. *Courtesy of Huntsville–Madison County Public Library.*

Jedge Daniel was a teenager who lived near downtown Huntsville in the mid-fifties when he first became interested in rock and roll music:

> *We always had music on around the house, including a lot of early fifties pop stuff, but I can think of two influences pretty early on. I remember Slim Lay, a local DJ for WBHP, playing Elvis as a country artist, although it was pretty obvious he wasn't singing country. My memory is that the first couple of Elvis songs didn't really create a buzz in Huntsville, although they were played pretty often. It kind of accumulated over two or three months and then, all at once, all you could hear was Elvis. You know you didn't really see the artists back then, you only heard them on the radio, so you'd have to use your imagination. I loved it, like most of the kids I knew who were my age. It was something just for me; it made me sit up and listen.*
>
> *It was pretty obvious that WBHP, a country station, didn't play black artists, so I just took it for granted that Elvis was white. We didn't have a local black station yet in 1955, it was a little before WEUP, so if you wanted to hear black music you had to listen to WCKY in Cincinnati or WLAC out of Nashville. What I do remember early on is that the DJs just didn't know where to place him. Sometimes, they would play a B side that maybe sounded more country. That happened here with "That's All Right Mama," where the DJs played the country-sounding flip side "Blue Moon of Kentucky" more often, at least at first. The rock and roll stuff was so different, I guess they were afraid their audiences just wouldn't get it, but they did.*
>
> *The other early memory I have is the first time I heard Little Richard singing "Tutti Frutti," I guess that was also in '55. I already knew and liked Elvis, but when I heard Little Richard, it all went out the window. All that early fifties pop stuff, Frankie Lane, whatever, that was the end of that!*
>
> *I started going down to the black business section of town down on Church Street, where there was a black-owned record store, I think it was called the Music Box. It was close to where you turned off Clinton onto Church, near where Channel 19 is today; it's all changed so much over the years. It was a little hole in the wall store right between several black clubs. The owner, I don't remember his name now, had the jukebox rights to these clubs; he'd save me some of the records he knew I liked, they were 78s, and sell them to me for a nickel.*
>
> *I had heard "Tutti Frutti" because a friend of mine had the record; I don't remember where he got it. I have to admit the first time I heard it I*

> *thought it was a woman singing. I thought, "Wow, what kind of name is Little Richard for a woman?" That song really set me on fire for rock and roll, and it still does fifty years later. At that point, it was more than just Elvis. A year or two later, the Sun Record tours began coming through Huntsville, and those concerts made me an even bigger music fan.*

Late Fifties Armory Shows

Jedge Daniel remembers sneaking into shows at the Dallas Street Armory in the late fifties and seeing many of the great performers of the time, including rockabilly pioneer (and role model for the Cramps) Charlie Feathers and His Musical Warriors, who may have had with him a stand-up bassist from Madison County, Jerry Huffman:

> *I don't pretend to remember all the groups that came into town on the Sun Record tours back then, but for those who liked rock and roll, it was a pretty big deal. There was a little advertising on the radio, but mostly it was just fliers tacked on utility poles, buildings, wherever, then it was passed on by word of mouth. All the concerts were at the Dallas Street Armory; that was really the only place back then for a rock group to play to a sizable audience. I didn't have any money, but a friend of mine and I had found a great way to get in. There was a broken window up high at the armory that never got fixed, so we would always climb up this hackberry tree by the side of the building, crawl out on a limb, step over onto the ledge and then enter through the window onto the bleachers that had been set up for the concert. It always worked!*
>
> *What's stood out in my memory after all these years is the excitement. Charlie Feathers and His Musical Warriors were great, and I really liked Warren Smith, who I thought, wrongly, was going to be the next big thing after Elvis. Jerry Lee Lewis also played here about a year after the Sun acts started coming through town. Let's see, Carl Perkins, Charlie Rich and Johnny Cash also came through here. Billy Lee Riley and the Little Green Men were one of my favorites; they were a tough group that could really rock. Oh yeah, Roy Orbison and his band the Teen Kings, they were a tight band with a good drummer, I can't remember his name, played here too. Orbison wasn't the ballad singer he later became; he sang a lot of fast rockabilly stuff and played a good lead guitar. They all put on a great show; really only Carl Perkins seemed to me to be uncomfortable on the*

stage. He looked as if he had made up his moves ahead of time and was a little stiff. Most of these guys would just set up and let go. Kind of like Elvis, they seemed to be having a great time.

The audience was sitting just a few feet away from the stage, which was pretty small and set up under the basketball goal at one end of the gym. Essentially, seats were placed on the court, and then they deployed the bleachers so you were right there with the performers. The noise just bounced around everywhere in the gym; it kind of enhanced the sound. They had, by today's standards, absurdly tiny amps, but their music sounded great in that setting. I'm glad I got to see so many of these guys early in their careers. It was exciting, you could feel something was happening; you weren't sure where it was going next, but it was fun to be there.

There was a lot of audience excitement, not Beatles-like screaming, but more like "hollerin" when someone hit a good guitar lick. There was always a bunch of guys—it was almost always guys not girls back then—hanging around the stage, we called them "gators," snapping their fingers and just eating up the music.

Oh yeah, one interesting thing about Jerry Lee Lewis was that, as I recall, he was pretty laidback the first time he came through. He had just released "Crazy Arms," and I distinctly remember him wearing a maroon sport coat and not jumping around a lot. He sat and played piano; sure, he moved as he played, but there was none of the jumping up and banging on the piano. The next time he came through, he had his act together with the crazy antics, hollering and all that.

I guess my favorite concert was the one that paired Roy Orbison and his band with Billy Lee Riley and the Little Green Men. Orbison's band, the Teen Kings, just rocked on stage, he didn't move around at all but the rest of his band was running and jumping all over the place. He played a great lead guitar on stuff like "Ooby Dooby" and "Go, Go, Go." The Little Green Men were the Sun Records house band and played a lot of studio backup, but they were a fantastic group live, one of the tightest bands I ever saw.

I know black artists played in town, but of course, during this time they'd be playing to black audiences at black clubs. I do remember sticking my head into the black clubs on Church Street—I didn't have the nerve to go in—and waving at the musicians playing and they waved back. I was thirteen or fourteen then. I guess you might say rock and roll was something of an equalizer, at least while the music was playing. Still, Huntsville was a small, segregated southern town in the late fifties, so there was that color barrier that couldn't be crossed. I do think music began to break down some of those barriers.

SHAKE IT OVER SPUTNIK

When the Russians launched Sputnik, the first satellite in orbit, the Americans rushed to catch up. In January 1958, the Redstone-made rocket Jupiter C carried the U.S. satellite Explorer into space. The caption of a postcard commemorating the Jupiter C and Explorer I reads, "The Jupiter Composite Re-entry Test Vehicle hurled Explorer I, the Free World's first earth satellite, into orbit. This remarkable feat was accomplished by the U.S. Army Ordnance Missile Command, Redstone Arsenal, only 83 days after ordered to try." Bursting with pride, the people of Huntsville swarmed to the square to celebrate.

Rockets and rockabilly converged in song when Billy Hogan and the Twiliters wrote and recorded (on Madison, Alabama's Vena label) "Shake It Over Sputnik" about the night:

Left to right: Jimmy Walker, president of the Huntsville Chamber of Commerce; Mayor R.B. Searcy; Stuart Jones, chief of the U.S. Army Ordnance Missile Command's Civilian Personnel Branch; and Dorsey Uptain of the Huntsville Industrial Expansion Committee, celebrating the launch of Explorer I, January 31, 1958. *Courtesy of Huntsville–Madison County Public Library.*

Well a bunch of brains from across the pond
Came to America to help our native sons.
On a stormy night nineteen fifty eight
Down in Rocket City history was made.
Well everybody went crazy, took to town
Sirens went wailing with a rockin' sound
The mayor of the city let down his hair
Someone's shooting firecrackers on the court house square
bang bang bang bang ah ah ah ahhhh!
Me and my baby stayed up late while the Jupiter C rocked into space.
Move over Mr. Monday, you gotta make room
Shake it over Sputnik for the rocket city moon.

Richard Penniman: Little Richard Attends Oakwood

Throughout this book, you will hear personal testimony of the influence Little Richard had on rock and roll in Huntsville, but when he lived here, he had left the rock and roll life behind. Richard Penniman came to Huntsville for reflection and religious education.

According to his biographer Charles White, author of *The Life and Times of Little Richard*, Penniman was on tour in Australia in October 1957 when he saw a fireball streak across the sky. Mistaking Sputnik's first flight for yet another sign from God that he should quit rock and roll, he enrolled at Huntsville's heart of Seventh Day Adventist life, Oakwood College (now Oakwood University).

Horace Rice saw Little Richard preach downtown during his time at Oakwood:

Little Richard came to Huntsville. He had converted to Adventism, so he would sing religious songs. They had what was called a tent effort in the spring, when the Adventists would set up a big tent and invite people to come. It was usually for a week. It's a revival, but they called it the tent effort, same thing. I found it inspirational, although I was confused because he was famous and he gave up the money. Of course this was in the mind of a ninth grader who didn't see the big picture. There was something admirable about that. Here he is coming to talk to us, and we considered him famous. And then, too, he was a minister and that was confusing.

> *Of course, back then we didn't know about the homosexual side, cause you dare not talk about that back then. I wanted him to be the rock and roll guy. The tent effort would come into the city. One tent was pitched near Gallatin, across from the funeral home on Gallatin and Lowe. All these musicians were with them.*
>
> *Our band had played out of his book, "Tutti Frutti" and all that stuff. When he found out we had this group called the Satellites, he said, "I don't do that anymore because that's the devil's music." He would talk to us like he was trying to convert us, because he thought that if we liked that music, then we were on the wrong path. But we just liked the popular music of the day.*
>
> *One thing was, he knew that life. White or black, if you were a rocker, you knew that life, then and now. But we didn't want that life. We wanted to be professional musicians, and in high school we wanted to be a good band, because, you know, then you're popular. You could play in the proms, junior high schools, and go to all the events, have a little celebrity. But he didn't know that's how we saw it. I stopped going to the tent efforts.*

Penniman's fame followed him whenever he came into town. Bill Brandon did not know him personally, "but I was at Willie Battle's barbershop when he got his hair cut. Everybody was gathering around trying to get a lock of it."

Chapter 3

Segregated City

Councill High School, the Grove and the Chitlin Circuit

Huntsville had all the ingredients necessary for R&B (rhythm and blues) and soul music to flourish in the fifties and early sixties: musicians whose gifts had been nurtured, a community that loved music and an active chitlin circuit boasting great traveling artists and energetic house bands. However, most of the people of Huntsville never experienced this scene because Huntsville's rock and soul music got its start in a segregated city. A white person was forbidden by law to go hear Ray Charles at Adella's Supper Club, or Howlin' Wolf at Biggun Seay's, or Duke Ellington at Alabama A&M. When Frankie Lymon and the Teenagers sang "Why Do Fools Fall in Love" at Councill High School, the audience was all black.

For Ivy Joe Milan's first interview with the Rockophiles back in the summer of 2006, we sat in a meeting room of the Huntsville Public Library with a big window looking out at the old abandoned Councill High School building. As Ivy told a story about being on the drum line, he looked out at the grounds and suddenly realized, "It was right here! We are sitting right on top of the football field!" The three Rockophiles present for the interview, David Lilly, Jim Cavender and Jane DeNeefe, realized in the course of this interview that we know basically nothing about African American life in segregated downtown Huntsville. Jim Cavender noted, "That's a whole period of time that's really gone unchronicled, that transition from segregation to integration. I know when I was in high school, Alabama history just stopped at World War II."

Councill High School sat at the west end of the area known as the Grove. For the musicians in this chapter, the Grove was a busy African American neighborhood in Huntsville just a short walk south from Big Spring and the black business district. Ivy Joe was the first musician to mention the Grove, as well as the active cluster of black businesses around the intersection of Church and Holmes. Bill Brandon, Horace Rice and the Crimes brothers offered more insight into life in the black parts of town back when Huntsville was a segregated city.

William Hooper Councill High School

Saxophonist Ike Rooks is better known now as the "Voice of the Bulldogs." Butch Lacey thinks of Rooks as "one of my favorite teachers. He was a master social studies teacher and a good singer and saxophonist and track coach. Talk about a Renaissance Man!" In a video interview for the William Hooper Councill High School Alumni Association, Rooks tells of the origin of the Councill High School football field:

> *Councill High School football field: the story behind the story. When I was in Councill as a student, the city dump, I'm talking about the trash pile for the city, was right next to the school. On a hot summer day when the smoke was blowing and the dead dogs were steaming up, it was rough. And I had to come across there because I'd be walking down the railroad track from Holmes Street and I'd come through the trash pile, and several times my shoes caught on fire coming through the trash pile. Then God bless somebody who eventually said, "This trash pile shouldn't be so close to the school," and they moved it somewhere. Then a group of people in the community said, "Let's get our own stadium." So they got together and raised money, and you could go over there to that field and you could see remnants of the trash pile still left, but they made a football field out of it and put lights out there, and that's where the Tigers played. And I say, on a cold winter day, even now, you can hear the Tigers coming out onto that field over there on the same spot. Although now, where the football field was, there's a library, so a transition from a trash pile to a football field to a library.*

The Grove

At one time, the Grove was a house named after the trees. In 1909, Huntsville's newspaperwomen the Clay sisters revealed the origins of the

The Grove. *Courtesy of Huntsville–Madison County Public Library.*

name (see Nancy Rohr's *Echoes of the Past*). In 1809, when Huntsville's founding big landowner Leroy Pope first bought the land that became the town, he chose the hill south of the spring for his homesite and got started building a house. But before it was finished, Pope changed his mind and decided to build an even grander house up on the bluff that overlooks the spring from the east, the house we know today. He sold the Grove to the Mannings, who left it to the Lowes. The Clay sisters describe the fancy parties held there, recounting the lacework of family names associated with the Grove, family names still reflected in today's street names. Back in its heyday, the Grove was a social center, staffed by enslaved people of African descent. The Clay sisters indicate the widespread acceptance of slavery among their 1909 readers when, casually, they call the fiddle players "all colored and home grown." The house was torn down in the 1920s.

By the mid-twentieth century, the grounds of the old mansion had become downtown's main African American neighborhood, with clubs that hosted some of the most influential musicians of the chitlin circuit, artists like Ray Charles, Wilson Pickett, Tina Turner and Bobby Blue Bland. A short walk from the Grove, past Big Spring and headed north toward the depot, was the heart of Huntsville's black business district, the intersection of Church Street and Holmes Avenue. B.B. King, Joe Tex and Howlin' Wolf are a few of the many artists who performed at downtown Huntsville music venues that were racially segregated by law.

Drummer Horace "Pap" Rice was born in the Grove in 1944. While he recognizes the many inequities racial segregation created in the Jim Crow South, he also remembers certain strengths of living in a cohesive African American community. Professionals, businesspeople, domestic workers, blue-collar workers and laborers all lived in proximity and knew one another's children. His house was on the southeast corner of Lowe at Gallatin, across the street from the hill baby boomers call "where the mental health center used to be" but which the real old-timers remember as the site of Royal Funeral Home and its neighbor, Adella's Supper Club. He shares his memories of growing up in the Grove and working for Adella Dale, who was called "A-dell" by family and friends.

> *Well, I was fortunate to grow up in the Grove because in that area there was this mixture of people—professional, blue collar, struggling people economically—and because of segregation many blacks had to live in that situation. But what was great about it was that you had this mixture of people from dentists, teachers, college professors, businesspeople and then persons who were maybe working on the arsenal and were struggling, so that diversity was the richness of the neighborhood.*

The Satellites. *Left to right*: Butch Lacey, Horace Rice, Frank McCrary (whom Lacey called "the most gifted of us all"), Lloyd Jones and Everette Lanier. *Courtesy of Horace Rice.*

In the fifties, paths didn't cross, things were rigidly segregated and everybody knew their place. As a young black kid, you didn't have to deal with processing how to relate to the white community.

My mother was the manager of the cafeteria at Councill High School, which was right there. After the Depression, my dad went back to A&M. And they had a building trade program, and he became a bricklayer. A brick and tile mason and a landlord. So economically, that was the basis for my background between my mom and my dad. Turner Street was named after my grandfather Jim Turner, who was a grocer; he had a grocery store there, Turner's store. And my other grandfather, Papa Will Rice, had rental property in Calvary Hills and around Winston Street and Arnett Street, in the Honey Hole.

Horace Rice played drums in a dance band at Councill, the Satellites. He spent time at Adella's Supper Club doing odd jobs. On Sunday afternoons, Adella would open up the club and clear the floors as a place for the neighborhood children to skate. Councill High held proms there.

The building was nice, real nice for the times. It was on the chitlin circuit, so all the big black bands that came through the South played there. They had booths at the front, and there was a bar. There was a private dining room for parties, weddings. And then you'd go straight back and there was this big dance hall. And to the right was where you'd check your skates out. And then you move to the right, sit on the bench, put your skates on. Other end of the room, a bandstand. Bobby Blue Bland, Ray Charles, Ike and Tina, all the big names came through A-dell's Supper Club

This is a little footnote. Before she owned it, it was owned by a man named Jeffrey Johnson. What's so unusual about him is that his house in our neighborhood was so modern, so out of sync with the other houses. He was a wealthy man because of his landholdings. He lived diagonally across from my block. I lived on Lowe before you hit Gallatin. But he was one of the premier black entrepreneurs because he owned a motel and he owned the Chicken Shack. That's the name that preceded Adella's Supper Club.

I don't know the source of A-dell's seed capital for that kind of business. Her husband was a retired military person. We called him Sarge. And she had relatives in Tullahoma, Tennessee. I just know that it was this lady bought this club, which was very unusual for female entrepreneurs, white or black, during that time, bought this club and it flourished under her. I left and went to Chicago when I went to college, and I was away about two or three years. You know we lived in a nice frame house, but it was all caught up in something called urban renewal. When I came back my parents had moved to another part of town, and the downtown area had changed.

But before that, because I lived in the neighborhood, I would wash dishes over there. And that's how I got to see Ray Charles, because at that age I couldn't go to the club. But they came early and rehearsed, and that's how I got to see these people. They rehearsed, and I went in to get their autograph and sat there and listened to the rehearsal.

I just remember being in awe as I said, "Mr. Ray Charles, I have some of your records." He was very nice. She [Adella] *said, "Ray, this young man plays with the Satellites." Then he said, "What do you play? What do y'all do?"*

And I said, "Well, we play these songs by you."

I had to do the floors before the sound check, and the sound check was right before the gig. I was there right before rehearsal, because when [it was] *sound check time, the two of us kids had to clear out because it was liquor sales time. I didn't meet Bobby Blue Bland, but I saw him at rehearsal. Yeah, Little Jimmy Reed, Bobby Blue Bland, Sam and Dave, Ray Charles, just at rehearsal. She didn't mind sometime if I put the broom down, went over and sat down.*

And there was the guy with his baton you know. You know, the early Bobby Blue Bland format. It wasn't big like a studio band. It was big for on the road, but not as big. A reed section, brass section and the famous heavyset guitar player, Wayne Bennett, and drums. That was the lineup. A-dell was always like this, she would say, "Bobby," because she knew these people by their first name, "this young man plays with a band called the Satellites, and he likes your music."

Although the Grove neighborhood has vanished, it could be brought back to life in public memory through good research and writing. Sooner than later is always the best time to collect oral histories and locate artifacts and ephemera. Ample public records exist for the area, from deeds and abstracts to urban renewal materials and more. This book cannot approach the depth the topic deserves, but a thorough study of African American life in this important Huntsville neighborhood from the town's first founding up to the civil rights period would be a gift to the city. It could begin with the congregation known as Huntsville African Church (later named St. Bartley's Primitive Baptist Church) founded in the Old Georgia Cemetery near the modern-day intersection of Governor's Drive and Gallatin Street.

The Grove was south of the courthouse square. Bill Brandon lived on what was known as "the north side of town," near the depot:

> *I lived right next to the train station. There was a place where they made neon signs; my house was back up behind it. There was this big tree in the yard. That old tree is still there now; if you head toward the train station, you'll see it. For grade school, I went to Winston Street, near where old Woody Anderson Ford dealership used to be. That area, on the black side of the tracks, was called the Honey Hole. It was a real rough neighborhood, kind of like Mason Court used to be. I don't know the name of the store where I bought records, but it was on Church Street, close to where I lived.*

Ivy Joe describes the central black business district between the two neighborhoods:

> *Well let me talk a little about the black business area of Huntsville, where the clubs were. I have some great memories of hanging around in that part of town. When I was growing up, the black district was on Church Street*

This 1963 view from the Times Building shows Holmes Avenue in the right of the frame, looking west. Also in this area: Uncle Sam's Pawn Shop, the Terry-Hutchens Building, the Nite Lite and Biggun Seay's. *Courtesy of Val Ginter.*

This 1963 view from the Times Building shows the old courthouse before it was torn down, as well as the Municipal Building under construction, with the treetops of the Grove in the distance. *Courtesy of Val Ginter.*

where Holmes Avenue crossed. It was a vibrant neighborhood, especially on Saturdays, which was the "kicker," the day when all the good stuff happened. From Dixie Food Market all the way down to Gay's clothing store, all of that was pretty much black businesses, black barbershops and two cafés with black clientele. The Nite Lite was right in there too.

On Saturdays, all the country folks would come into town to buy stuff and relax after working hard in the fields all week. Church Street would be crawling with people "like ants on sweetbread," with all kinds of things happening. There were two cafés, the Busy Bee and the Blue Front. They were pretty big and were always packed on the weekends. They served bottled beer and soul food; you know, fried chicken, pig's feet, collard greens. It was a celebration after a week of hard work.

The area was also called Holmes and "N" Streets in a derogatory way, so you can imagine what the "N" stood for. There was also the Sweet Shop on the corner of Holmes and Church that I loved. Mr. Prince, a white guy, ran the Busy Bee, and I don't remember who ran the Blue Front. People were constantly going back and forth between them. There was also a club on Holmes Avenue called the Nite Lite where we played several times. We were probably too young, but they'd let us play our set and then leave.

The Chitlin Circuit

Bill Brandon describes some of the clubs of Huntsville's chitlin circuit and tells how he got started singing:

> *Yeah, there was the American Legion, and upstairs was a club we called Biggun Seay's. I remember seeing guys like Howlin' Wolf and Joe Tex there. Then there was a place across town called the Chicken Shack, where I saw the Falcons, when Wilson Pickett was with them; they were just known as the Falcons then. And Ray Charles, the cover charge was two or three dollars. It was also called Adella's Supper Club. It was near the Royal Funeral Home, and across the street was a Dairy Queen–type place, and then Dr. Hundley's dentist office was nearby. The way I remember it, you'd start at the top of the hill, and as you went downhill, there was Adella's Supper Club on the right. It was a pretty narrow street; we used to fly down the hill on our bikes. That was a dangerous thing to do, but we didn't think about it then. It was just fun. It was close to where the old white swimming pool was and Big Spring Park. It may have been Gallatin Street. You'd see placards on utility posts and walls; it seemed as if everyone in the neighborhood just knew about what acts were in town.*
>
> *I didn't start off singing. My first encounter with a band was playing guitar. I started with a group called the Comets; we played around in high school. Eventually, I joined up with a group from Gadsden, actually a group of teachers, called the Thrillers. I think the leader was Floyd Donald; he owned the black radio station down there. He also taught music out at what used to be Councill Training School, which was out near Alabama A&M. Thomas Stewart was on trumpet; he taught music in Pell City. Bill Harris played keyboards and taught at Carver High in Gadsden. J.C. Garvin played bass. Howard and I were probably the only nonprofessional people in the group at the time.*
>
> *We got together on weekends. I was playing with the Comets at the time, and the Thrillers had seen me play. One night at Biggun Seay's, their singer didn't show up, and I happened to be there. So they said, "Man, why don't you come up and help us out?" I lived down the street, so I ran home and got my guitar. We started playing, but we couldn't just play instrumentals all night long; somebody had to sing something. Floyd Donald said, "Can you sing?" It hit me then, and I said, "Yeah, sure!" The first song I did was "Rock Me, Baby," by B.B. King. I guess I was about sixteen or seventeen, just high school age. I was probably too young to be in there. As I mentioned, I'd been practicing at home in front of the mirror, you know, pretending, so I just started singing.*

> *After that, I sang with whatever group I was with. At that point it was a lot of Big Boss Man Jimmy Reed stuff, songs like that. It might have been twenty or thirty people there. I was so caught up in my chance to sing, I had no idea, really. The Comets eventually busted up, and I got with the Thrillers. They used to play down the street here at the VFW; that's where Charlie Ray first started. Big Stigger, Little Stigger and a lot of other good musicians used to play there. First it was the Huntsville Club, then it turned into the VFW. Used to be a Turner's Store behind there.*

Ivy Joe talks about his early teenage years living in downtown Huntsville and attending Councill High School:

> *For a while we lived right up on the hill, Hooper's Alley, remember where the Caucasian swimming pool used to be? South Central Bell had a place there, and the municipal building is there now. It used to be a really high hill, and we lived up on the hill, and we could look out and see all the people diving and stuff in the Caucasian pool. The black pool was over by the Scruggs Street Community Center, where the aquatic center is now. And actually, integration caused the closing of the swimming pool.*
>
> *You know, you eventually find out you're poor. When I first got into the school band at Councill, my family bought me this brown drum at Sam's Pawn Shop for about fifteen dollars. It was where the Heritage Club is located today. Well, I had my brown drum and was looking forward to marching in the Christmas parade. I remember Mr. Hall saying, "Ivy Joe, you can't march in the parade with that cheap brown drum." He wanted me to get some nicer drums (I think it was a "blue pearl" set or something like that), but we just couldn't afford it, so he put me on the cymbals. I had one important thing to do: clash the cymbals at the right time during the National Anthem. Actually, I kind of liked the cymbals; you could twirl them and keep time on them during the drum solos ching, ching, ching, ching. Actually, I never learned to read music but could pick up the drum beat real quickly. I'd always placed myself in the middle of the drum line so I could hear what was going on and could imitate whatever was being played. I really never understood what they meant by the rudiments of drumming, but give me a second and I could play anything.*
>
> *Rock and roll got my attention with a movie I saw with Chuck Berry and Bill Haley and the Comets. I remember that Bill Haley had that little curl on his forehead. There were other bands playing during the movie, and it was really great. I liked Chubby Checker and Little Richard, definitely.*

Above: Uncle Sam's Pawn Shop, *Courtesy of Huntsville–Madison County Public Library*.

Below: Home of an unknown drummer, from the Urban Renewal files. *Courtesy of Huntsville–Madison County Public Library*.

The Chicken Shack was not far from where the library is today. It was close to that grove of trees where the doctors' offices are, kind of diagonally behind where the Jim Williams Aquatic Center is now. The black people's swimming pool was also in that area. There was a street on the hill where the Mental Health Center used to be called Gardner Street, and the Chicken Shack was sitting right there in what I call the Grove. There were a lot more trees there back then before all the construction.

The Chicken Shack had red siding and an outdoor porch with a brick wall surrounding the porch. I used to sit outside on top of the brick wall. I wasn't old enough to go in, but you could hang around and hear all kinds of good music. A lot of good bands, when they came to town, they usually played at the Chicken Shack. There were so many! Let me see: Hank Ballard, B.B. King, Bobby Blue Bland. Probably more bands than I realized came.

The good black bands and singers would perform there when they were in town. Now that I think about it, the Chicken Shack may have been the same thing they called Adella's Supper Club; it was called both at different times. I'm getting some names mixed up. What I do remember is the Chicken Shack was a real juke joint for black people, and they always had a good band on the weekend. I was too young to go in during a band, so I hung out on the porch. I could hear everything just fine. That was as far as I could go.

When a black businessman named Jimmy Johnson first built the new building for his nightclub, he playfully named it the Chicken Shack, causing some in the neighborhood to dub it the Royal Palm Chicken Shack. When Adella Dale bought the business, she changed the name to Adella's Supper Club. Around the Grove, the club was known variously as A-dell's, the Chicken Shack and sometimes the Royal Palm. Most people remember it as the Chicken Shack.

The Crimes Brothers

Twins Richard and Russell Crimes lived in a neighborhood just east of the Grove, at the lower end of Adams Street, now the site of Huntsville Middle School and the open expanse split by Townsend Avenue. Richard Crimes recalls:

We went to Councill High School. We lived on Kranse Alley. It ran into Greene Street. They were block houses all connected in one little strip. That was behind the Elks, the one on Franklin Street. There was a little community right there, but then the city bought all the property over there in the seventies and late sixties. My grandmother had a house, but she had to sell it and move.

We were born here, but in the migration of the early fifties, black people were going north to Chicago to work in the auto plants. We went to Chicago for a while. When we returned, we were in the fourth grade through the sixth grade at Councill. In the sixth grade, we started out with the band. Mr. Edwin Hill was our band teacher. We rented our instruments. I was on bass clarinet, and Russell was on baritone horn.

Then we moved over to Calvary Hill, where we had Mr. William T. Robinson. That's where Mr. Clarence Gandy was the one who opened my eyes to jazz. Sat me down and put on this record, "Misterioso" with Sonny Rollins and Thelonius Monk, and the fireworks blew! We played funk and played some jazz too. I guess I was maybe in the tenth grade.

Motown was popular then, so we were always sitting around piddling with Motown. In middle school, as long as we didn't disrupt anything, Mr. Robinson would let us stand in the corner and make a little noise. His favorite song was "Will Johnny Learn to Play," and it had a dance routine. DUH duh DUH duh, dada DUH and then you'd kick. Kids always want to do the common stuff, as they play instruments. As a kid, you want to kinda do the popular stuff.

We had good instructors musically when we went to Councill, under Mr. James Wilson. He was a graduate of FAMU. [Pronounced "fam-you," Florida A&M University is famous for its marching band.] *He would not let us play "Hot Cha" by Junior Walker until we transcribed the charts. We played all the horn parts.*

Russell*: We liked Maceo and James Brown. When they'd have a dance at Councill High School, they'd always have James Brown on the box. Nobody was sitting down; they'd jump straight up. It was just popular.*

Richard*: During high school, we played up at Biggun Seay's with Howlin' Wolf and Arthur Conley. They wanted to take us to Chicago with them. We played with Little Johnny Taylor and Rosco Robinson. Then the Invaders, Ted Walton, Spot* [Willie Butler] *and Bo Dollar pulled us down to the Nite Lite.*

The Invaders

Russell explained, "The Invaders were musicians that had come into Huntsville from Birmingham. A lot of musicians there came here. We had a lot of places to play, and things were better here in Huntsville than in Birmingham. Bo Dollar, Curtis and Burley Marshall, those were all Birmingham people coming into Huntsville. They're here today because there were more gigs here."

Horace Rice could see why some musicians chose Huntsville over Birmingham:

> *One thing in Birmingham, a lot of black bands couldn't play in white clubs. Redstone Arsenal was the difference, bringing in people from all over, in the military. People had started getting used to some semblance of integration, not for political reasons, but it was just practical reasons. A lot of time they just wanted good music. It wasn't so much what the band was composed of, because when the 55th Army band, when they played, black, white, Latinos, and people got used to that, because it was about the sound.*

One day, Horace saw members of the Royal Nigerian Air Force in the whites-only park.

> *There's something else that isn't about music but it seems relevant. The Royal Nigerian Air Force did simulation training in Huntsville. They had these bright blue uniforms with crimson. Since they were a former British colony, they trained in England and they trained in America. And this was the sixties now—a lot of the Nigerians who had lived in England had white wives. When they came to Huntsville for six months, they had to have a weekend. They had to be able to go out with their wives. So a military policeman would accompany them to Big Spring Park, and sometimes they'd put their robes on, their boubous and their kufis. You'd look through the fence, and there's this Afro-blonde kid, and a white wife, and a very dark-skinned West African, in the sixties, in the white park. But I couldn't go to the white park.*
>
> *And these are things that Huntsville had to get used to. It blew us away in terms of thinking about race. Because this wasn't just a foreigner. This was a black African with a white wife! And a light brown kid with Afro-blonde hair. I'm riding my bike past the park, and the first time, I went home and told my parents about it. Sometimes I would go by and just look. And they had MPs. These are things that other cities wouldn't have had to process. Huntsville was getting used to white foreigners, the Germans, the Austrians. Now here was a group of foreigners they hadn't anticipated, black foreigners who were also pilots.*

Chapter 4

Rocking Redstone and the 55th Army Band

One can hardly overstate the impact of the U.S. Army and Redstone Arsenal on Huntsville's culture and economy, and that includes the music. The notion that the United States Army is the largest employer of professional musicians in the world is easier to imagine when you explore the symbiotic relationship between Redstone Arsenal and the musicians of Huntsville in the 1960s. Huntsville would still have had music without the army, but it would not have seen such diverse influences, and local bands may not have seen such steady work. Redstone Arsenal brought musicians and music lovers from every region of the United States, infusing the local sound stew with fresh ideas. Not just soldiers but whole families came here to live. Retired military people, who liked living near the commissary and other amenities, brought their musical interests and record collections. Huntsville's unofficial town band, the 55th Army Band, employed highly skilled professional musicians. Four different clubs on the arsenal hired local bands to play regularly: the Officers' Club, the NCO Club, the Enlisted Men's Club and the Teen Center. President Harry S Truman had ended racial segregation in the United States Armed Forces in 1948, so racial integration was a standard practice on Redstone Arsenal.

In this section, soldiers stationed at Redstone (and their civilian drummer friend) share stories of music and life in early sixties Huntsville. Californian Dan Pollock found the opportunity to immerse himself in an authentic experience of the music he loved most: rhythm and blues. Fred Wesley, who had played trombone for Ike and Tina Turner and Hank Ballard in his late teens, and who became famous later as a pioneering arranger of soul and funk horns, found out when he arrived that he was transferred to Redstone Arsenal for his jazz trombone abilities. Val Ginter came to teach in the missile school and then stayed to work for WAAY television, continually developing his jazz accordion skills through collaboration with other Huntsville musicians. Horace Rice was an observant drummer around town.

Dan Pollock: Blues for the White Boy

Dan Pollock of Oxnard, California, joined the army in 1963 and was transferred to Redstone Arsenal in 1964. Before the army, he had played with a regionally acclaimed rhythm and blues band in California called the Mixtures. The name was a play on the racial composition of the band, which had African American, Latino and Caucasian members. The portion of his memoir *Blues for the White Boy* that chronicles his Huntsville days is published on the web. The quotes and stories that follow are based on the web-published portions of *Blues for the White Boy*, as well as e-mail correspondence with Dan Pollack and the memories of his fellow musicians.

Dan recalls:

> *I didn't think my kind of music would be found downtown. It was 1964, and* The Twilight Zone *was still cranking out episodes on the tube. After a few hours of being among Huntsville's citizenry, I'll swear I saw Rod Serling leaning against a building smoking a cigarette! I was scared to go off post. Whenever some of the guys from my unit would go clubbing downtown, the next day, I'd grill them about the bands they heard and to describe the music the bands played. That was a feeble effort because these guys weren't going down there to check out any music. They were down there to party, get drunk and hopefully get lucky. One guy remembered hearing a song he liked, "Pipeline," a surf hit of the period.*

He didn't expect this, but Dan formed lasting friendships with Huntsville musicians like Frank McCrary, Sonny Davis, Carl Jackson, Lloyd Jones, Horace "Pap" Rice, Ted Walton, E.W. Wainwright Jr., Everett "E.J." Turner, Pat Greene and Fred Wesley, among others.

One night, Dan told Horace Rice of his frustration with "not being able to get back in the alley with a guitar." Horace "didn't have to talk very hard to convince me into going down to the Elks after he finished his gig so I could hear some guys around town play at an after-hours jam session. When his gig was over, I helped him pack his drums and we headed off post toward town in his car. I was really anxious to see if this scene lived up to his vivid description."

Not only did it fulfill Dan's expectations, but they also let him sit in, according to his memories in *Blues for the White Boy*:

> *They were playing a lot of songs I knew already, including, Bobby Bland's version of T-Bone Walker's, "Stormy Monday" with Lloyd Jones on piano and doing the vocal. I had almost all of Wayne Bennett's nuances in the song and I wanted to do that one first but they called it as the first slow tune of the set. I'll just have to convince them to repeat it when I get up there. It seemed like they took forever to call me up and when they finally did, I asked them to repeat "Stormy Monday" and they complied. I brought Lloyd in just like Bennett did for Bland and when I retarded the introduction on the D augmented chord and hung on the last note for Lloyd to start the first verse, "they call it stormy Monday but Tuesday's just as bad," Lloyd turned to me and said, "you're hired" and I was allowed to finish the set with them. I thought Lloyd was kidding but after the gig, he sat at our table for the longest, telling me about gigs that were coming up and how my guitar would really fill the void. This time I was hired in a black band because I could play, not because I just happened to own an instrument.*

Fred Wesley: The 55th Army Band and "Uncle Sam's Army"

Note: Although several of the musicians interviewed have talked about Fred Wesley, the Rocket City Rockophiles have not interviewed Mr. Wesley personally. All Fred Wesley quotes in this section are from his autobiography, *Hit Me Fred: Recollections of a Sideman* (Durham, NC: Duke University Press, 2002).

Fred Wesley thought he must have been assigned to Redstone Arsenal by mistake. He tells his story in his autobiography, devoting most of the chapter called "Uncle Sam's Army" to his time in Huntsville. When he received his orders to Redstone Arsenal, Alabama, Wesley writes, "I just knew it was a one-horse country town full of unhip, non-jazz-loving people," so he assumed that meant he was doomed to play reveille at "an ammunition dump." When he arrived, he saw signs about the Marshall Space Flight Center and the United States Army Missile Command. His job was to play trombone for the 55th Army Band.

The way Wesley remembers it, "being in the 55th Army Band was not like being in the Army at all. Duty for me was reveille, clean-up, coffee, big-band rehearsal (!) and that was it. We were finished by about 1 PM most days except Fridays." Friday was missile school graduation day for "military people from countries all over the world studying at the missile school." He describes the 55th as "a diverse band, any way, consisting of Rebels, Yankees, Jews, Italians, Germans, Puerto Ricans, me and Floyd, and plain ol' white people, some with wives of equally diverse ethnicity." Fred Wesley and Floyd Cotton "were the only two black people in the big band."

Before arriving at Redstone, Wesley had found out the hard way that the army had a rule against its musicians playing non-army gigs, so he was surprised that playing outside gigs appeared to be the norm among his new band mates. The band as a whole also played in a variety of settings. "We would play gigs at the general's house and get paid as if we were a civilian band." They played parades and events around Huntsville "for local goodwill. We called these non-pay GI gigs. We had to wear our uniforms and be spit-shined and all that."

After Wesley had been in the 55th for about six months, Floyd Cotton "joined the FBI or something," leaving Wesley the only African American left in the big band that played in the off-base gigs. Sometimes they played civilian gigs for "upscale, affluent society types who, if they were prejudiced, kept it under wraps." But the band "was already aware of the potential for a racial incident, and was on guard at times." When they were hired to play at a party in Arab, Alabama, a town "renowned for not having any black residents or even allowing blacks to pass through," Wesley at first decided he just wouldn't go. But his band mates wouldn't hear of it and unanimously agreed that "either we all did it or none of us did it."

Wesley recalls, "My eyes were opened to the fact that music creates strong bonds of friendship between people of all races, religions and ethnic backgrounds. We had all kinds represented in that band, and not one of them let me out of their sight throughout that whole evening. It was a love and togetherness I hadn't experienced before." He felt that "music brought people together that night, and music had done it before and will do it again. If there is someone you don't like or someone who doesn't like you, take them to hear a big band. You'll like each other better afterward."

Fred Wesley may have had good reasons to be concerned about Alabama in those days, as well as about playing a gig in all-white Arab, but his experience at Redstone expanded his view. The 55th Army Band was a whole new thing for him because "I had never had a friend who wasn't black like me before. Don't get me wrong. I didn't turn white or anything. I just learned that you have to get to know a person—black, white, blue or green, old, young or in between—before you determine whether you like him or not." Beyond that, he says, "I was also filling the gaps in my musical education."

The 55th Army Band

The 55th Army Band was no ordinary band. It could play all the usual stuff, like the Sousa marches you would expect. But for Wesley, what set the 55th apart was the band's immense big band jazz book. In jazz, a "book" is a sheaf or collection of jazz sheet music or "charts" designed to give musicians the basic structures of a tune from which they are expected to improvise. The charts show basic arrangements, such as the chord progression or "changes," and they note where each improvisational solo takes place. Back in the days when charts shared among friends were usually copied by hand, to have a "thick jazz book" meant having an abundance of music for songs that other bands probably didn't play. A great book deserves a great band. Wesley gathered that someone, somewhere, understood enough about big band jazz to bring some of the best jazz musicians in the army to one place, Redstone Arsenal, to play in the missile school's band. Fred Wesley remembers:

> *The band was kicking, without a doubt the best big band I had ever played in. This was what I dreamed it would be like to play in Count Basie's band. The drummer was world class. His name was Henry Okstel. A health fanatic. He had chops, he could swing real hard, and kicked a big band like Buddy Rich or Louis Bellson. Tom Zale, from Cleveland, was the piano player. Classically trained. Good comper, good soloist.*

Wesley goes on naming band members in every section, giving a sense of cultural and regional diversity within the band: "a Philadelphia Italian" who "did all the house-rocking stuff," a "self-proclaimed redneck coon-ass from Covington, Louisiana," on baritone sax, a "hippie-type and serious be-bopper from San Francisco…" Wesley's book goes into much greater detail and contains photographs and names of more of his band mates from the 55th.

Drummer Horace Rice first met members of the 55th Army Band when he sat in with the Alma Haygood Quartet. Drummer Greg King considers Alma Haygood "a great musician" because "her personality flowed out of her fingers and into the music." Horace Rice recalls:

Alma Haygood was in a quartet with Bob Henderson and James Milner. I met Bob and Alma at the Elks Club in 1964. Bob, Sergeant Henderson, played sax in the 55th Army Band. We played jazz standards and light pop songs because the music was tailored to the audience.

By '65 and '66, things were open then as far as integrated bands playing in white clubs and different venues. If you saw the 55th coming down the street, it would be trombone section: white black white black, trumpet section, dadada. They were a role model for the town. This was the town's band! And people in music circles knew the stars in the 55th. Some of these guys were career military men who had moved up to the rank of sergeant, Sergeant Henderson and Sergeant Warnet Warner. Some were master sergeants, and some were regular sergeants. Stationed in Germany, or Fort such-and-such, and then Redstone. In the 55th, the level of musicianship was so high.

They were ambassadors for the military, too. Even if you didn't like race mixing, they provided a contrasting picture to how ludicrous [segregation] *was, because you like this band, and they're integrated. Since these guys were military, they always had military identification, and when they came to clubs, and if they had a problem with policemen, once they showed their IDs it would temper how the policemen would treat them. For one thing, their first call would be to the MPs at Redstone, and a Redstone MP would come, so a Huntsville policeman wouldn't want to say, "Well, I arrested him because he was playing in a band with a black guy."*

VAL GINTER AND THE FOUR SOUNDS

When jazz accordionist Val Ginter arrived at Redstone Arsenal in 1963, he, too, went in search of the sounds he craved and found jazz peers among downtown Huntsville's African American community. Eventually, Ginter formed a quartet called the Four Sounds with some army friends: James Milner on string bass, Danny Romero on trumpet and civilian Horace Rice on drums. When Romero's duty was up, Fred Wesley replaced him in the Four Sounds. After the army, Ginter went on to work at WAAY-TV.

After attending radar school at Fort Monmouth, New Jersey, the army sent me to Redstone Arsenal to teach "common block" material to Nike Hercules students in the U.S. Army Ordnance Guided Missile School (USAOGMS).

I grew up in Chicago in a Polish American household. WGES was all Polish until around 7:30 p.m. At 7:30, they had The Lithuanian Hour. *And then at 8:00, all of a sudden it became a black station, with Sam Evans and* Jam with Sam. *Sam Evans used to do this Purple Grotto routine.*

The Four Sounds, in the woods. *Left to right*: James Milner, Horace Rice, Danny Romero with trumpet, Val Ginter standing with accordion. *Courtesy of Val Ginter.*

But I play the accordion, and in Chicago, every major broadcast operation had one or two or three be-bop accordionists. And I got into that quite early. I got interested in jazz accordion as early as 1951. The exact moment was one day when I was sick in bed with the flu. I was around twelve or thirteen years old. This one Saturday, they brought up Charlie Ventura and his Bop for the People entourage featuring Jackie Cain and Roy Kral. Mousey Alexander was on drums. You might say I was hooked. After becoming an avid reader of Down Beat *magazine, I began to realize that the whole color thing was a major issue in the music business.*

Dave Brubeck was once quoted as having said "Nuts!" to a club owner when he tried to get Brubeck to get rid of a black bassist. I thought that was really cool, and I thought: Someday, I'm going to do that. And I did, in Huntsville.

When the army sent me to Huntsville, I noticed that the black NCOs were very friendly to me. And they would invite me to their houses to have dinner. This changed any negative ideas I may have had toward blacks, having grown up in a "white" city.

Everybody had their own musical experience depending on where they grew up. When I got to Huntsville, the native [Madison County] *white musicians were all playing rockabilly and that Ace Cannon, yackety sax-type stuff. The native black musicians were playing soul and jazz. So I naturally migrated toward the black musicians. And they were the ones who asked me to play with them.*

Also, the 55th Army band was loaded with people from Kenton, Herman, James, Basie, Crawford. So I played with both white and black jazz musicians in Huntsville. But I also played a Polish wedding with a hillbilly band, because the sponsors of the wedding didn't want black musicians playing a Polish wedding. So instead of hiring my group, they hired a hillbilly group and asked them to hire me for the Polish side. I wish Horace Rice had played that gig, because he was one of the best polka drummers I had ever heard. He knew the meters.

We played intermission music for Clarence "Gatemouth" Brown. But his accordion player, Clifton Chenier, I had heard, did not like playing in Alabama, so Gatemouth used me during his act. He and I got along very well together musically. I learned a lot from Horace Rice, James Milner, Danny Romero and Fred Wesley. They taught me little tricks of the trade in playing.

Chapter 5

Finding Common Ground

Blues, Jazz and Soul

That the sixties were a dynamic decade of change is evident by several measures. The civil rights movement and the legal changes it brought challenged the codes and customs that had ruled the South since at least the end of Reconstruction. By the end of the decade, the space program would achieve its goal of humans walking on the moon, something that seemed brazen and outlandish in 1961 when Kennedy proposed the Apollo program. Television broadcasting brought news and entertainment into homes, spreading culture and information at an unprecedented rate. Increasingly, women were resisting the confines of their societal roles.

Huntsville was caught in a unique bind. Alabama in the 1960s had the most famous segregationist governor in the country, George C. Wallace. But Huntsville was a forward-looking federal town, home of NASA, with an important army missile base. After a long series of focused and well-organized peaceful civil rights demonstrations (best chronicled in Dr. Sonnie Hereford's documentary video *A Civil Rights Journey*; see also Hereford and Ellis, *Beside Troubled Waters*, and Sheryll Cashin's *Agitator's Daughter*), Huntsville quietly desegregated public facilities before the Civil Rights Act of 1964. The local civil rights story is too complex to recount here, but there are two key points. For one, the civil rights protest efforts in Huntsville were sustained, creative, peaceful and on the side of justice. Also, Huntsville's business leadership and police chief chose to stand on the side of federal law, unlike other places in the state, where local leadership sided with the Ku Klux Klan. Huntsville had struggles, and there was plenty of racial prejudice, but the officially sanctioned mass violence seen in Birmingham, Gadsden, Marion and Selma did not happen in Huntsville. Schools in Huntsville were the first in the state to integrate peacefully. A famous photograph shows George Wallace reading a Birmingham newspaper with the headline "Huntsville Defies Wallace."

Val Ginter remembers how one locally beloved business handled the transition:

> *There was a family called the Bergerons who had the Kentucky Fried Chicken franchises in Huntsville. Whenever I got hungry, I'd drive as far as the Tennessee River on the Parkway to find a fast-food place where I hadn't eaten before. Most of those places had a sign that said Whites Only. And on the side or in the back, was a little window that faced out onto the parking lot that said Colored.*
>
> *Well, when you walked into Bergeron's Kentucky Fried Chicken, everybody walked in the front door. They had a reception room with sofas and a big coffee table loaded with* U.S. News and World Report, *the* Christian Science Monitor, New York Times, Time, Life, Nation, New Republic, Ebony, *etc. And after you placed your order, everybody of all races sat in those sofas and read the magazines and newspapers as we waited for our breaded gizzards and hearts, and all the other great stuff they served. It takes innovators and progressives!*

Still, everybody knew which were the black or white music venues. The music itself was colorblind, appealing to the full spectrum of listeners, and musicians were working across racial lines more than ever before. In Muscle Shoals, for example, black and white musicians recording together had become a normal thing. But the personal feelings of many everyday people were slower to change, giving rise to strategies like the private club to preserve the racial status quo.

Bill Brandon went to Muscle Shoals to record "Self-Preservation," a song written by Huntsville guitarist Willie Butler, with Brandon's input:

> *I think it was '64. With Quin Ivy. Jimmy Hughes, you know "Steal Away," we used to go over to his house and play, kick a little about, try to write something together. The first thing we recorded was "Self-Preservation." After that, I got hooked up with the rest of the guys: Jimmy Johnson on guitar, David Hood on bass, Roger Hawkins on drums, Barry Beckett and Harrison Callaway, we used to hang. Harvey Thompson played sax. This was a studio band, the session band. Jeannie Green and them used to sing backup. I was in Muscle Shoals doing my own thing. I*

met good people when I was there, like the musicians Spooner Oldham and Dan Penn who wrote "Rainbow Road.

[Working with white musicians] *wasn't unusual for me because music was a common ground. The only time I saw discrimination was when Fred* [Wesley] *and I were on the road with the Mastersound. We saw quite a bit of that, because there were places where we would stop to get gas, and they'd have one sign, colored here, and then whites over here. But other than that, I don't recall ever having a problem. And I played a lot of places, a lot of places.*

Private Clubs

When Val Ginter started playing music around Huntsville, he noticed that the white bars and the black bars he frequented approached race relations differently:

The white bars in Huntsville were all clubs. You had to have a membership card. That way, they could keep out the black patrons. Only black musicians could come in. And during the breaks, the black musicians had to sit in the kitchen. But I thought it was interesting that whenever I entered a black club as a patron (which I did because of the music), I was immediately surrounded by four or five blacks who wanted to buy me a drink. And I would have company as long as I was in that club. When I played at the HiFi Club (a white club) with Gatemouth Brown, the black musicians all had to leave the room during the break. Needless to say, [white] *patrons would call me over to sit and have a drink with them. I'd just politely decline. And we'd go out to the car where we kept a flask.*

I started playing in Huntsville in the summer of 1964. My father had boxed my accordion and sent it down to me, and I was practicing one night in my apartment at 315½ Franklin Street. This guy, drummer Joe Williams, heard me practicing through the window, came upstairs and told me I was booked into the Holiday Inn in two hours with a bassist and a drummer. "You won't let me down, will you?" That was really my first professional gig in Huntsville. Then I met Danny Romero, and he introduced me to Pap [Horace Rice] *and Milner. And I started playing with them.*

I played with the Val Ginter Trio that night that Joe Williams booked me. As I was driving up to the Holiday Inn on Memorial Parkway around 9:00 p.m., I saw that the revolving sign in front said: "In the lounge: Val Ginter Trio." I

Left: Four Sounds poster, handmade by Charlie Nork. *Courtesy of Val Ginter*.

Below: Private club card. *Courtesy of Val Ginter*.

Mount Charron Country Club
HUNTSVILLE, ALABAMA

Special Guest Card

Highway 231 - 431 North to Nashville

Entertainment Nightly Go Go Girls

Telephone 852 - 7437

Val Ginter
Name

Good Any Time

Date

Signed

almost ran my car into the drainage ditch alongside the highway. Jane Couchois would book the trio a lot. And I did my own booking. There were a lot of telethons, and we played in schools and prisons. We also played some convention work. The trio was originally all white, but then I met Pap and Milner. And it didn't bother Jane because she was from California. Her husband was a physicist or something with one of the large military suppliers.

The Mule Inn and Napoleon's Nook

Percussionist Duke Way tells a story from this transitional period that gives a sense of how arbitrary the private club arrangement could be. After the final show of a little theater production, the cast and crew went to the director's regular bar to celebrate the birthday of one of the cast members, who happened to be African American:

> *Tables were pulled together to make one long table, and, since it was also Drew's birthday, we gave him the seat of honor at the head of the table. For a short while, the atmosphere seemed friendly enough and quietly chatty, with country music playing on the jukebox (which should have been a dead giveaway). Before long, the owner came over to the table, leaned over Drew and quietly asked for his membership card.*
>
> Sidebar*: Back in those days, Huntsville was blue-lawed to the hilt, and pubs could only exist as "private clubs," members only, and their guests, which, in practice, meant pretty much anybody that walked in the door. It also gave pub owners the excuse to exclude anybody who was, oh, say, the wrong color.* End sidebar.
>
> *With only a slight tinge of sadness in his voice, Drew announced to the table: "Okay, people—I gotta go."*
>
> *The whole table got up and left. Not a show of resentment, simply going with the local house rules. Somebody suggested Napoleon's Nook, a club on Bob Wallace Avenue famous for its festive atmosphere, and we all agreed.*
>
> *It was a totally different ambiance when we got to the Nap's Nook. The management was delighted to see a whole herd of people coming in, and the patrons, too, waved their glasses and shouted miscellaneous greetings and words of welcome. Party! The waitress even wished Drew a happy birthday (she'd heard us mention it) and took his order first.*
>
> *The Nook partied on as though nothing out of the ordinary had happened. On the whole, it more than made up for Mule Inn.*
>
> *The next day, Joe dropped in at the Mule Inn for his customary after-work beer. The owner set it before him and said, "Mr. Dickinson, I'm really sorry about last night, but you know, a lot of my customers have a problem with nigras."*
>
> *Joe smiled and said, "Oh, that's okay—we moved the party to Napoleon's Nook, no problem at all. We had a* great *time. There must have been thirty or forty of us. We drank and we drank! I must have spent fifty bucks just by myself."*

The owner's eyes glazed over as his blown mind wrestled with the math. Last time I looked, the Mule Inn, located on Meridian Street just north of Oakwood Avenue, was an abandoned building.

The Wesley-Davis Mastersound

Fred Wesley and Sonny Davis decided to put together a serious band. They started off playing regularly at Charlie Ray's Amvets Club, everything from specially arranged Beatles songs to R&B classics like "Tighten Up." Two soul singers, Pete Lou and Bill Brandon, worked up dynamic duets inspired by Sam and Dave. In *Hit Me Fred*, Wesley describes the band:

Pete Lou and Bill had to perform on the floor where everyone was dancing. We had only one mike—and that came out of a taxicab—you had to hold the button down for it to work. The singers had no problems, but Jack had to hold the button down for me to play my solos, and I had to hold the button down for him to play his solos. This was okay, but I got a lot of spit on my hand when he played his flute solos.

The band shifted to the newly renovated Elks Club on Pulaski Pike, a place "geared to the more affluent members of the black society in Huntsville. Professional people like doctors, lawyers, teachers, scientists and engineers who worked at Redstone or Marshall Space Flight Center."

They called their band the Mastersound "because of the fact that we grew out of a variety of sounds—jazz, blues, R&B, Latin, gospel—and created one dynamic, master sound." Drummer Teddy Caldwell was "equally fantastic at playing jazz and straight-ahead as he was at playing funk and R&B. His only problem was that at times he would get excited and get carried away and overplay sometimes. Of course, we not only approved but also actually encouraged that sort of thing."

For their grand opening, the Elks Club booked the Ike and Tina Turner Band, a band Wesley considers "a model of how to play with confidence and energy." He worried that his new band would be intimidated by having to follow such a "devastatingly entertaining" show. But the Mastersounds "hit the stage like a band possessed. During the half hour we played, Teddy broke his sticks, Burley busted a speaker, Sonny pulled blood blisters on fingers he'd been playing on every day. Both Pete Lou and Bill sang themselves hoarse. Experiencing the Ike and Tina Turner Revue firsthand was the best thing that could have happened to the Mastersound."

According to Wesley, the Mastersound almost came to blows one night over whether to play James Brown's "Cold Sweat." Wesley was adamant:

> *I had heard "Cold Sweat" and was very unimpressed with it. It was not on par with the material we were playing. It had only one change, the words made no sense at all and the bridge was musically incorrect. I wasn't about to abandon our upscale style and selection of music to sink to the level of a little honky-tonk sissy singer and sound like every other band up and down the pike. Our uniqueness was what made us.*

Wesley had to decide whether to reenlist in the army or make a full-time go of the Mastersounds. He chose the band and "got honorably discharged just in time" because people were being shipped to Vietnam without warning. He recalls, "I'll never forget how it hit us when the always jovial Sergeant Petracco—who had been in the army for twelve years, always in bands, never in combat—was suddenly shipped out to Vietnam. There was panic throughout the band. If he could go, anybody could go."

James Brown: The Godfather of Soul

For Jack Robbins, "My first concert was James Brown at the Coliseum, and it's the kickin'est band I've heard to this day. They were three hours late, but by the end we were nothin' but smiles." Terry Barkley heard James Brown on the radio before seeing him in the TAMI show. To fully appreciate the vitality James Brown inspired in local musicians, it would be best to view a video clip of him singing "Please, Please, Please" at the TAMI show, because that performance was widely imitated in 1960s Huntsville, and audiences loved it. Toot Snoddy recalls, "The Tiks did a lot of James Brown music, and Bobby Grant was especially good at the James Brown stuff."

Like most people, Terry Barkley heard James Brown on the radio before he saw him move:

> *We certainly listened to WEUP, the local black station, whenever we could to hear good soul music. Actually, the first time I ever heard James Brown was on WEUP. The white stations weren't playing any James Brown until the mid-sixties with "This Is a Man's World" and "Papa's Got a Brand New Bag." In 1965, I saw James Brown doing all his moves in the TAMI show movie at the Centre Theatre on Triana, and that made a big impression.*

Bill Brandon met Brown in Huntsville and again in Birmingham:

> *I studied him so I could emulate him, you know. You had to on our side of the tracks. I remember seeing him out there on that hard concrete. We were interviewed together in Birmingham one night before a show. We were doing a live promo thing on the radio station WENN. I recall it was the first time I'd ever seen a man kiss himself. He was an egotistical maniac! When the Mastersound broke up, Fred Wesley went with James Brown. He needed a trumpet player and he knew about Russell Crimes, so when he came back home, he got Russell to go with him. Huntsville has had a lot of good talent.*

Terry Barkley was also impressed by the James Brown show at the Coliseum:

> *That may have been the* best *live concert I've ever seen; it was incredible. He was accompanied by a whole band with strings, three set drummers who could play like nobody's business and his backup singers, the Famous Flames. I couldn't have told you the names of any of the drummers, but they were incredibly talented. JB was in his prime, and he did all his moves and routines just like in the TAMI show. I have a picture, a little Polaroid shot really, of the band after the show. They were dressed in their short red tuxedo coats and looked really sharp, really good. The rhythm section wore short gray tuxedo coats.*
>
> *From the beginning to the end, it was "wow!" Fully choreographed, something exciting always going on. The Famous Flames were dancing and singing backup. They had a Temptations thing going on while James did his moves up front. The white bands, like us, mostly stood on the stage and played and sang, you know like the Beatles, but here everyone was moving, all kinds of stuff going on every second. When he did "It's a Man's World," the strings came in and it sounded great. You know, the Coliseum really was a terrible place for a concert because of the poor acoustics, but James Brown sounded fantastic.*

Ivy Joe Milan attended the Coliseum show and learned the moves for his own band:

> *Our James Brown stuff was exciting. We'd even do it when we played at country clubs. I'd get on one foot, scoot across the floor like James, fall down on one knee, bringing out the cape.*

I saw him out at the Coliseum. Mitch Montgomery got me backstage before the performance. Actually, he was really a good guy to take time to talk to me. For some reason, I remember James's and the Famous Flames' hair. He didn't have a full conk; it was more a case of him using a straightening comb and bumping the front up and twisting out a curl. The Flames had full conks where they used an acid-based solution to straighten their hair with a full sculptured pompadour on top. I guess you could also call it a pompadour look. I remember it being popular with black guys during the fifties and early sixties, but I think it had been around for much longer. The hair was straightened to the point of having a hard, shiny finish to it, with a pompadour piled up in the front. At various times James Brown, Jackie Wilson and other performers wore conks.

The concert was great. He had an eighteen-piece orchestra with a couple of drummers. One thing you tend to forget is that he usually opened his concerts with a set of his instrumental music. He was a killer on drums and could play guitar too. A lot of the B sides of his singles were instrumentals. It seems to me that he opened up with a woman singing, then followed that with Bobby Byrd, one of the Famous Flames, singing a song or two, then James Brown would come out and play a couple of instrumentals, finally the announcer would introduce James for the main show. It was a pretty lengthy show, but it was great from beginning to end. Russell Crimes, who played for him later, talked about how demanding he was on his band. Sometimes you'd see James pointing a finger at someone and singing, "I got ya, uh huh, I got ya." James Brown was letting a band member know he'd missed a beat or note and was being fined.

Russell Crimes tells the story of how he came to play in James Brown's horn section under the direction of Fred Wesley:

Fred Wesley had a band here, and we had a band, and he used to come and hear us play. Then Fred went to play with James Brown. Well, Bootsy, with Bootsy's Rubber Band, used to play with James Brown, but they got mad and quit, so Fred had to come up with a band right quick, so he called me, and I said yeah, why not? So I went and caught the bus, rode the bus and walked into the hotel and met the fellas and that was it. I had to sit behind the stage and read the music for two or three weeks. Fred wrote the charts because we had a gig coming up at the Apollo. So I'd be sitting way up here backstage reading the music.

> *Most of the stuff we played when I was with James Brown, it was real simple. The key thing was the "one." We watched him when we were playing, and he'd be moving, so you see you got to watch him all the time. See, he might make a certain move and you got to hit it when he does that. Bass line ain't got nothing to do with that. It's time. You got to watch him. You just got to keep your eyes focused all the time.*
>
> *In the studio, he'd just hum out a melody and then he may say, "Fred you do something with that," you know. Most of the time Fred would do that before we get there. He'd hum the chorus to us and then we'd play it and he'd put the horns on top of it like that. Basically, when you travel a lot you basically play the same song basically over and over again. He might throw something in there every now and then, that's what the deal is. So you got to watch him at all times. He was real strict at the Apollo. See, the audience was mostly black and they expected more out of him.*

Curtis Marshall remarked, "Now, when one brother went with James Brown, I expected the other to go too. You should have heard them play. The two of them were seamless." Richard Crimes explains, "Russell went to play with James Brown, and I went off to Saigon. Plus, I was married, so I guess that had something to do with it."

Chapter 6

The British Invasion

The Baby Boomers Meet the Beatles

When the rock and roll onslaught known as the British invasion hit the U.S. airwaves, "post-Beatles bands" broke out all over Huntsville. The irony of Huntsville's garage band explosion of the mid-1960s is that the music that sparked it was introduced to Huntsville's teenagers by bands that, in turn, were inspired by the same rhythm and blues that had already flourished here locally.

Little Richard called John Lennon of the Beatles "one of the greatest entertainers black, white, red, brown or yellow," but he has told the story more than once that "John used to travel with me to Hamburg, Germany" when they played "at the Star Club, and we was there together when they sang [he sings] 'How could I dance with another? Woooooooo!' And you know they got that from me."

Lennon himself once explained, "Of course there is a lot of great white music these days, but it is still black music. Man, I'll never stop acknowledging it. Black music is my life." Like Elvis with his new interpretations of rhythm and blues songs, British bands like the Beatles, the Rolling Stones and the Animals brought a new spin and energy that attracted teenagers in a way the older versions had not. The British invasion time period, roughly 1964 to 1966, saw a prolific growth of garage bands.

Larry Byrom remembers the night he decided he wanted to play rock and roll:

> *Yeah, the night I saw the Beatles on* Ed Sullivan. *That was shocking! Because I had never even heard of 'em, and I didn't know what the deal*

> *was, and all these girls were screaming. And I thought wow! That's really neat, they're wearing these nice suits and they're gonna get the girl. And they were so good, they really sang great, along with the force of their songwriting. It really opened up a new world for me and changed everything. That took me out of Dixieland jazz and trumpet. At the same time I was listening to Chet Atkins and copying his records and learning to play "Yankee Doodle" and "Dixie" at the same time. That was a big deal. Seeing the Beatles did it for me.*

Joe Hardin's dad bought their family's first Beatles records:

> *My father thought the Beatles were an interesting "novelty act," so he actually brought the first Beatles record into the house. He was sorry he did that, I think. I went to sleep every night with a radio next to my bed, memorizing lyrics from the songs I heard on WAAY and WBHP.*
>
> *Like many kids of my generation, it was the Beatles that personalized the desire to be a musician. I remember distinctly thinking that this was music focused on me, especially once I saw them on* Ed Sullivan. *All the other music I had heard I enjoyed and played, but it was made for other people: my dad, my uncle, etc. The Beatles were playing music for me.*

The Beatles also changed the direction of Terry Barkley's musical interests:

> *Yeah, the Beatles did it. I remember when they first appeared on* Ed Sullivan. *There was a lot of buzz at school even before they appeared. We had already heard "I Want to Hold Your Hand" and "She Loves You" and read in the paper about the concerts, screaming and riots even before they came to New York. When they landed, all the craziness got covered on TV and in the newspapers. We were primed. Sunday night the family was sitting around the TV when* Sullivan *came on. He introduced the Beatles. I had never seen them, I'd just heard and read about them. They made a real visual impression, the matching Edwardian suits, cool guitars, screaming girls and their names being flashed up on the screen since we didn't know them as individuals then. I'd never seen anything like that; it was like "Wow! What's going on?"*
>
> *Actually, I wasn't totally into rock and roll before that night. I was thirteen or fourteen years old, playing in the school band at Westlawn Middle School. I kind of liked Elvis, surf music and rockabilly, but I wasn't quite there yet. Seeing the Beatles did it. I remember my brother*

and me making eye contact during the performance, and something passed between us like "we can do that!" I was playing snare drum in my middle school band, and my brother was a clarinet player in the Butler High band, but we were sure we could play rock and roll. I think I remember my parents being scandalized, the long hair and everything, at a time when guys were still wearing crew cuts, but we thought it was cool. You know, with the matching suits they kind of looked like bankers do today, but back then it was dangerous. I guess that made them even more appealing. I had started playing drums the year before, so I noticed Ringo doing his hair flip and pictured myself sitting there playing for a rock band.

The Beatles inspired youngsters all over the city to start rock bands. Terry Barkley and his brother J.R. started the Shandells:

Not long afterward, we decided to try to start a band, which eventually became the Shandells. As with so many other groups, we began by going down to Sears and buying really cheap Silvertone guitars and amps. Back in '64, there were only two music stores in town. Robbins was the big store downtown. Jackie Robbins, whose father owned the store, was a schoolmate and friend and was in the Shandells for a while. We backed him up, by the way, on "Please, Please, Please" out at the Madison County Coliseum; we ripped off the Tiks on that one. Anyway, Doyles Music in Five Points was the other store. Dad took me there, and Jimmy Corder (he later owned Corder's Music and played drums around town) sold me a bottom-of-the-line three-piece Ludwig drum set and some cheap Japanese cymbals.

Ludwig was Ringo's brand. After the Beatles debut, all the local drummers went to Ludwig, if they could. We really followed the Beatles while they were in America in New York, Miami and Washington. A lot of garage bands sprung up within weeks and months after that, but most of them never got out of the garage. One of the early accomplishments of the Shandells was that we became a working band. You know, we had actually dabbled a little bit with surf music before the Beatles, stuff like the Beach Boys, Jan & Dean (the surf movies and all that), but after the British invasion, we pretty much lost interest in that.

We were all Butler High School students, one of many mid-sixties teenage bands in the area. My brother [J.R. Barkley] *was lead singer and played rhythm guitar. He later on played with the Hi-Boys and with another group, Colfax. His wife and he also had a band for almost twenty years called Flash, what I'd call a company band; they'd play mostly for*

Deltones, including James Butler, *far right*, whose 1970 band played the entire *Tommy* rock opera to sold-out crowds at Huntsville High School. *Courtesy of James Butler.*

corporate parties and get-togethers. Getting back to the Shandells, we had actually talked about being a surf band and were going to call ourselves the Macahas, which was supposedly a beach in Hawaii—I don't know if it really is—but think about it, a surf band from the mountains of north Alabama! Anyway, after the Beatles hit, we became the Shandells. I don't know what a Shandell is, but there were a lot of "dells" music groups back in those days. We were together for about four years. We broke up when my brother was drafted; he was the lead singer, and the band was kind of vocally built around him.

We played a little bit of everything. Old rock and roll, blues, R&B, British invasion. Of course, the British stuff was mostly reworked black R&B sent back to America. Then we reworked it again back in America, songs like "Tobacco Road" that the British group the Nashville Teens released in America. We liked everything from Jerry Lee Lewis to the Moody Blues—when they were actually playing something like the blues, you know, when they had Denny Laine. The Zombies were another group we liked. We played a really good mix of all the music types that were around in the mid-sixties. We had a lead guitar player, Pat McQuiston, who was actually a country guitarist who could play anything; he was as fast as greased lightning! One of the funny things about the Shandells was that we prided ourselves on how fast we could play a song. When things got a little slow on stage, we'd just say, "Let's pick things up." Then we'd get into a key and let it rip. We'd take a three-minute song and play it in two and a half minutes. We thought we were one of the fastest bands around! Those up-tempo songs were fun.

Pat, our guitar player, later played locally with Tony Mason and stayed pretty much in the country vein. He was an Alabama country boy, and he admired Chet Atkins. I do remember on our second record that he learned

Shandells record on the Woodrich label. *Courtesy of Kip Shepherd.*

Terry Barkley, late 1960s, in a field with his drums. *Courtesy of Terry Barkley.*

to play the fuzz tone. In all, he was really talented. Tim Gray was our bass player, and he played with a number of other bands later on. The late Mike McQuiston, Pat's cousin, was brought in as a keyboard player and second singer. We called him "Gorgeous George" because he did the Jerry Lee Lewis stuff really well; he had the peroxided hair, cherry red shoes and could do things like playing while standing on top of the keyboards, playing with his feet, you know. He was a real showman, whereas my brother was essentially a stand and sing type. Mike could really grab an audience. Jack Robbins was also in the group for a brief period.

We played anywhere we could find. The guys in the established bands like the Tiks and Hi-Boys were a little older and had been together since the early sixties, initially inspired, probably, by the surf craze. They could get gigs around town pretty easily. It was tougher for the newer groups, but there were places to play.

We were kind of the house band, or maybe one of several that played a lot at the Redstone Arsenal Teen Club, which was across the street from the old Officers' Club. It was only open on weekends. We got a chance to try out our stuff there. It certainly didn't pay much. You'd get a piece of the door charge, maybe. High school kids from all over town could go there and listen to local groups. I saw most of the major Huntsville bands play there. That was really a home for us.

We also had a pretty regular gig at the Aquatic Club on Jordan Lane. They had a bar downstairs for older folks, but upstairs, especially on the weekends and during the summer, it was a hangout for teens. Different bands would come in, but I remember we played there pretty regularly. We also played at the Dallas Street Armory and the Madison County Coliseum.

I literally grew up in the Shandells. My first everything as a teenager happened because I was a drummer in a popular local rock band. I was a terrible athlete and something of a geek, and playing drums in the school bands and in rock groups defined who I was. I dated the prettiest girls at Butler simply because I was a "cool" rock drummer.

Adrian Clift recalls, "All the bands I knew in the early days played mostly on the arsenal, school dances or for special show/dances at National Guard Armories in Huntsville and Decatur or Athens. Combos would start out at the Teen Club and later graduate to NCO and Officers' Clubs and

Precious Few, first practice, with a drum that still says the Tempest. *Courtesy of W.C. Cowles.*

Precious Few in New York City. *Left to right*: W.C. Cowles, Jack Mentzel, Mike Couchois, Jimmy Gentry, Doug Shaw and Pat Couchois. *Courtesy of W.C. Cowles.*

special parties held here and there. I distinctly recall walking across to the Officers' Club one night and gawking at the Hi Boy's Fender equipment and polished style."

Larry Byrom compared the styles of the mid-sixties bands he played with: "The Tiks did James Brown and Young Rascals stuff like 'Grooving.' Precious Few was Wilson Pickett, 'Ninety-Nine and a Half,' you know, blue-eyed soul. Good Times was the Beatles, *Rubber Soul*, 'Drive My Car,' stuff like that."

Despite widespread interest in the Beatles, there were some, like Tommy Graham and Jack Robbins, who professed fondness for the Rolling Stones. Richard Crimes said of the Beatles, "I liked them, but I was into Motown, R&B and Junior Walker, you know, in that era." Russell Crimes agrees: "I liked the Beatles, and I watched them on *Ed Sullivan*, but the instruments weren't that interesting. I was really into horns. That's what caught my attention." Richard goes on, "I wasn't so taken by the Beatles also, because I was really into front line horns and arrangements. From our side of the fence they just didn't appeal to our peers and to us. We had a little radio in the kitchen, and we would sit and listen to what they would play, and I like the Beatles, but I was doing the R&B. We always do the R&B and the funk thing."

Rocket City Records

Several Huntsville bands made records, some under the guidance of Woody Richardson of Woodrich Records, including the Shandells, according to Terry Barkley:

> *We did two singles with Woodrich Records, a regional label owned by Woody Richardson from the Muscle Shoals area. It was a mom and pop operation that usually recorded country and gospel. But after the Beatles and the whole rock and roll explosion, a lot of small labels tried to get some of that action by recording local groups. We were one of several local groups that cut records with Woodrich. I know the Hi-Boys and the Rocks did, and maybe the Tiks too.*

Woody Richardson told the Rockophiles, "I started writing songs in the cotton patch. Country music was all I knew. I was about fifteen years old. Before he died, Perry Como recorded one of my songs." Richardson is happy to report, "I'm still getting paid on Marty Stuart."

Richardson worked at NASA in the sixties, recording mostly gospel, country and bluegrass music on the side. Some of the Huntsville bands he recorded besides the Shandells are the Rocks, the Poor Souls and the Shadows, pressing from three hundred to five hundred 45 rpm records for the band to sell. "We had a set price, we got thirty-five dollars an hour," he explains. "That stuff is expensive. This is analog equipment!"

Richardson's first Huntsville recording was in 1960: "This fellow named Buddy Hughey played semi-rock, semi-country, a song called 'The More I Learn to Care.' Buddy also recorded on a label called Cherokee Records" on Oakwood Avenue.

Terry Barkley shares more details of his recording experience with Woodrich:

> *They were 45s, so they'd have an A and B side. The first record was "Smile at Me, Baby," with an instrumental, "To the Woods, by the Swuft Wulf" on the flip side. You can google "Shandells, Inc." and get more information on the songs. We were just the Shandells on the first record, but became the Shandells, Inc., on the second. The second record was "Say What I Mean" with the flip side, "Just Cry." Both songs were written by Barkley-Gray, my brother, J.R., and Tim Gray, our bass player.*
>
> *Anyway, back to recording our records, Woody usually recorded his performers in Nashville, so we went up to a place called Music City*

Left: The Continentals' record "Charleena," sung by Jimmy Gentry, Spot label. *Courtesy of Kip Shepherd.*

Right: The Rocks' "Because We're Young" on Woodrich. *Courtesy of Kip Shepherd.*

Recorders close to Music Row. Right off, we were introduced to Scotty Moore and D.J. Fontana, who, I believe, were part owners of the studio. Being children of the British invasion, worshipping at the altar of the Beatles and Stones, we had no idea at first who they were. We finally found out they played guitar and drums, respectively, for Elvis Presley, and did that make an impression! I remember there was a ratty old set of drums in the studio with a brown and white calfskin on the bass drum head that I refused to play on. I actually ended up playing on my own set.

After the recording session, I was walking down a hallway filled with pictures of music stars, looked up at a picture of Elvis performing somewhere, and there, in the background, was D.J. Fontana playing that brown and white calfskin head drum set. Little did I know! Anyway, we did our first record there, and it was challenging. Woody had only booked us for three or four hours, and that wasn't really enough time to set up, run sound checks and do a bunch of takes. It was, essentially, a couple of takes and "that's a wrap," pretty much "live" in the studio. We were recording in four-track, so the drums, bass and rhythm guitar were playing on one track with the lead singer, backup singers and the lead guitar on the other three. Since three instruments were playing together on one track, there were lots of opportunities to mess up. Our playing just wasn't as good as it could have been if we'd had more time. You know, as a musician looking back on sixties records, even those made by big name artists, you can hear a lot of mistakes with modern digital technology. Those records were designed to be played on the radio with a "wall of sound" coming at you, and you couldn't hear the individual instruments well. Listen to them on CD with headphones, for example, and you can hear all kinds of things going wrong that you never knew were there. That was certainly the case with our recordings.

Shandells Record in Muscle Shoals

Our second record was done over at Quinn Ivy's studio in Sheffield. It was a typical small studio; a cinder block building with egg crates on the studio walls to pad the sound. It certainly wasn't like the big operations at RCA or Capital Records. However primitive it was, Quinn Ivy produced some major stuff: Percy Sledge recorded "When a Man Loves a Woman" there, and Lynyrd Skynyrd did their demo tapes there and then hawked them around to the major studios. It had some good music history. It was a better session for us, all in all. But I'll tell you one thing: we never made any money off our records, but that was typical.

We had several different managers. A couple of DJs managed us at different times. Sonny Limbaugh, who was pretty big locally at the time, managed us and a number of other groups for a while. WAAY radio/television was owned by M.D. Smith in Birmingham, and the DJs had pretty much total control over what rock and roll was played in Huntsville on the Top 40 each week. Of course, the big national acts were always on the list, but they would slip in local talent from time to time. Obviously, it was good to have a DJ managing you since they could put you on local radio. They could also get you gigs; a store opening sponsored by WAAY needed a band and the DJ just happened to have a band!

My memories of these guys were that most were pretty sleazy. I'm sure there were exceptions. They always had stage names like "Johnny Dark" or something like that. I don't know about Sonny Limbaugh's name. Another of our DJ managers was Johnny Gann. The important thing was you could get some airplay. Turn on the local rock and roll station in the sixties, early seventies and you would occasionally hear the Shandells, the Rocks or the In. Today, with programmed music, there's little chance for local groups to get local radio airplay. On the other hand, the Internet has opened up different kinds of opportunities to get noticed. Maybe it's better, maybe it's not; it's a different music world today. I do remember that the local DJs in the sixties were free to have some fun, since they could play whatever they wanted. That made them exciting to listen to.

Val Ginter clarifies, "Robert Limbaugh's stage name was 'Sonny Limbo.' Mitch Montgomery's stage name was 'Johnny Dark.'"

The Rocks and the In

The only Rocks band member I knew well was Skip Atkins. They were popular here in the late sixties, and like us, they played around the area and cut a couple of singles on Woodrich Records, etc. There were other labels that local groups signed with. The In recorded on Hickory Records. They were another late sixties, early seventies band. I only knew George Vail, their drummer. He was another of the local drummers, and I followed all

The Rocks' "Love City" on Gold Master. *Courtesy of Kip Shepard.*

of them. I liked the In because they played a lot of Byrds stuff. I remember seeing them at the Epic Club in Five Points covering the Byrds really well. Both bands were in what I'd call the second wave of post-Beatle bands that became popular in Huntsville during the late sixties; I wasn't as involved in the Huntsville music scene then, so I didn't know them as well as I did the Hi-Boys or the Tiks.

London Deal Falls Through

London Records came to Nashville looking for American talent and signed a number of groups, including us. Our contract with London was through Dino Productions, based in Nashville. They had a good reputation when we signed, they had managed Bobby Vinton, among others, but that was to soon change, and they went belly-up in a big mess not long after signing us.

We went back to Nashville to record at, I think, the Gold Nugget Studio. London liked our first single, "Smile at Me, Baby," so we recorded it again. Interestingly, they gave us the lyrics for a B side entitled "Can't Find a Job"—they were simply terrible*—and told us to build a song around them, which we did. We were really excited because London was a major label; the Rolling Stones recorded on London, which was a huge deal to us. The Moody Blues were on London too, as well as some other major British groups. We bought subscriptions to* Billboard *and* Cashbox *and waited for our name to appear on the Top 100 lists and zoom up the charts! We waited and waited.*

There was a big brouhaha at Dino Productions right after we recorded, and it collapsed with a lot of accusations and claims of scandal and corruption; somebody, I think, absconded with the funds. There were plenty of lawyers, and our parents got involved. None of the groups Dino signed for London, including us, ever got anything released; we were dropped like a hot potato due to all the legal problems. No other label wanted anything to do with anyone involved with Dino Productions. So the single was never released. I remember listening to an acetate of it, and it sounded pretty good. Nothing came of it, and frankly, everything began to play itself out for the Shandells after that. My brother went to Vietnam, and I graduated from Butler and went off to college and played in both marching and rock bands.

Chapter 7

Ivy Joe and the Snowballs Integrate Huntsville High School

Huntsville's public schools did not desegregate all at once but gradually over the years. It was September 1963 when Sonnie Hereford IV enrolled in Huntsville's Fifth Avenue School, the first African American child to enroll successfully in a previously all-white Alabama public school. Joe Hardin remembers the scene when he showed up to school that day and other moments during the effort to desegregate:

> *One very strong memory is from the first day of third grade, when I walked through a line of National Guardsmen to go to school at Fifth Avenue Elementary. The Guard was there because the first black kids were coming to school that day. I remember getting out of the car and walking through the line of Guardsmen. I couldn't really tell what it was about because I was only ten, but I knew that everyone was upset.*

A few specially selected African American students broke the ice in previously white schools like Huntsville High before the bulk of the black students arrived. The class of 1966 was the last graduating class of Councill High School. Ivy Joe Milan, Russell and Richard Crimes and the rest of Councill's student body were dispersed to the city's formerly all-white high schools: Huntsville, Butler and Lee. Richard Crimes reflects that the transition was stressful but went more smoothly than he and his twin brother Russell expected:

> *So, we were at Councill in our sophomore year, junior year they closed the school due to desegregation, and trauma set in. We're going from a relaxed, comfortable environment over to Huntsville High, where some may want us and some may not, and they were ahead of us in a lot of ways, because they had things, I mean technologies and teaching methods that we didn't have at Councill because we didn't have the resources, you know. So we got through that and we joined the band. We were both in the band over there. I played bassoon in the concert band under Mr. Sloan.*
>
> *We graduated in '67, and Ivy Joe and the Snowballs, they were top of the charts at the school. We competed with them in the talent show. We were doing James Brown. We came on stage and played and every eight or sixteen bars, somebody would unplug our amplifiers, and we'd turn around see what's going on, get going again and they'd unplug it again. But that's probably the worst thing I can say about Huntsville High. I mean, the transition went fairly smoothly. But during the sophomore and junior years, we were doing our version of the chitlin circuit. Technically, they were shot houses. They would hire us and we would go in there and play.*

Russell Crimes adds, "Our band was the LBJs, for Lively Blues and Jazz. After that, we called it Alla Breves."

When Tommy Graham got to Huntsville High School on that first day of full integration, he observed the arrival of two of the new African American students:

> *I started the band the Snowballs at Whitesburg Junior High School in eighth grade. It was the same school year Kennedy was assassinated, was that '63? So it was probably '64. Our whole band decided we'd learned soul music, because soul music was coming out and we just loved it. Then we went to Huntsville High School. I remember that first day, because there were National Guards when we pulled up. And I saw Ivy and Mary. They were the two I saw. And I remember Ivy, the National Guards were gonna walk him up into the school, and Ivy said, "No, I'm good." And he walked in by himself. 'Course everybody was shunning him and standing back. There was a ten-foot area around everywhere he went. Nobody would speak to him. In fact, it got pretty bad.*
>
> *I was in the lunchroom having lunch. He sat at a table, and he was by himself. I walked over and put my tray down, and he looked kinda startled, you know, and I put my hand out, and he shook my hand. Now, I might as well have been black myself. So now everybody's sorta turned on me.*

I said, "Yeah, I heard you can sing real good." He goes, "Yeah." I said, "Well, I gotta little band." He says, "The Snowballs, I heard about you guys, you play soul music." I said, "Yeah, but we can't sing it. We're learnin' all these songs but we can't sing it so we're just doing instrumentals. We're rehearsing Saturday, you wanna come by?" Ivy asked me where I lived, and I said in the southeast on Weatherly Mountain.

Ivy said, "Uhhhh, I don't know…" We had to change it from Saturday evening to Saturday noon cause he was uncomfortable about coming down to southeast Huntsville after dark. But I mean, we just hit it off, instantly. So Ivy Joe and the Snowballs were born.

Ivy Joe describes a time they won a contest at The Mall:

We played "Monkey Time" to win the contest. Major Lance had just released it as a single. It was probably more R&B than rock and roll, but everything seem to fit together on the radio back during the sixties. I danced the monkey while singing. People loved it. The contest was at the west entrance of the mall, facing Pulaski Pike. We set up on a stage right in front of a store, and people were walking by as we performed. Whenever we did "Monkey Time," people would stop; it just brought the house down.

I was at Huntsville High School when we formed the band. Basically, at first it was Tommy Graham, for sure, Bobby Martin and Eddie Roberts. I can't remember all the initial group members, it soon changed a lot. These guys asked me if I could sing. Of course I said I could!

Oh yeah, I was always singing and dancing like Jerry Butler at home. So I didn't hesitate to say I was a singer, and we started playing together. Eventually, Chris Couchois came in to play drums. I can't remember who played drums before Chris. The group eventually ended up being myself, Chris Couchois, Mike Byrom, Tommy Graham, and after Eddie went to college, Billie Brown joined. We got together in late 1966 at the start of school integration in Huntsville, and the band lasted until 1968.

After a while we began to get good, but we really got tight playing at Steve's Lounge. It was off Conception Street near the old farmer's market on Cook Avenue. You turned off Pratt Avenue at Orchard, and take a left as soon as you crossed the railroad tracks and there was Steve's. Now that I think about it, Steve's was really called the Peppermint Lounge. We knew Steve, I've forgotten his last name, so we always called it Steve's. It may have gone by that name at some point, but I believe it was the Peppermint Lounge when we played there.

Well, I guess we were such a hot item that they overlooked our ages. They really loved us. We actually played a lot of country and western stuff there. I remember singing things like Ray Charles's "Here We Go Again" and "Wolverton Mountain." I could sing "Wolverton Mountain" with that country twang. Now that I think about it, we did a whole lot of Ray Charles at Steve's too, but if you played at Steve's, you had to be able to do all the country stuff. You know, growing up I also listened to WBHP a lot and liked country music, so it wasn't too hard to pick up on it. Of course, we did a lot of James Brown in other places. Our James Brown stuff was exciting. We'd even do it when we played at country clubs. I'd get on one foot, scoot across the floor like James, fall down on one knee. Yeah, we did the complete James Brown routine: falling on your knees, bringing out the cape.

We performed a lot at the Epoch Club over on Andrew Jackson Way during 1967, which was our big year, but we really played all over town. The Epoch was run by a guy named J.C., I can't remember his last name, but he worked a lot with young local talent. The club later changed its name to the Unique Teen A-Go-Go. I think eventually Books as Seeds was in the same building. We could really play a little of everything, I'd already mentioned playing country stuff at the Peppermint Lounge but we really liked playing sixties soul and R&B, you know, Otis Redding, Wilson Pickett and especially the Young Rascals. We'd do other things too, early BeeGees and even some stuff from Sergeant Pepper *like "Lucy in the Sky with Diamonds." Arthur Conley's "Sweet Soul Music" was popular then, and I remember singing that all the time. We also liked the Drifters' "Up on the Roof" and "Under the Boardwalk."*

Thinking back, I remember Mitch Montgomery from WAAY radio wanted me to leave the band and pursue a solo career with him as my manager. I refused to leave the Snowballs, they were the ones who reeled me into the band and helped me get started. We had good camaraderie. I wasn't going to leave them.

Most of the time the black-white thing was fine. We'd mostly play to white audiences in the area. We also went down to the University of Alabama and Auburn for performances. I do remember we'd often open our concert from behind a curtain, the crowd would roar when the curtain was drawn back and there was this black guy singing with some white guys. They'd start clapping and stomping their feet! We might start off with something like "I Feel Good" or "In the Midnight Hour" or maybe with whatever was popular at the time from the Young Rascals. We weren't limited to just white or black stuff; we'd cover almost anything currently

Above: Ivy Joe and the Snowballs at the Epoch Club. *Courtesy of Billie Brown.*

Below, left to right: Tommy Graham, Ivy Joe Milan, Chris Couchois and Billie Brown. *Courtesy of Billie Brown.*

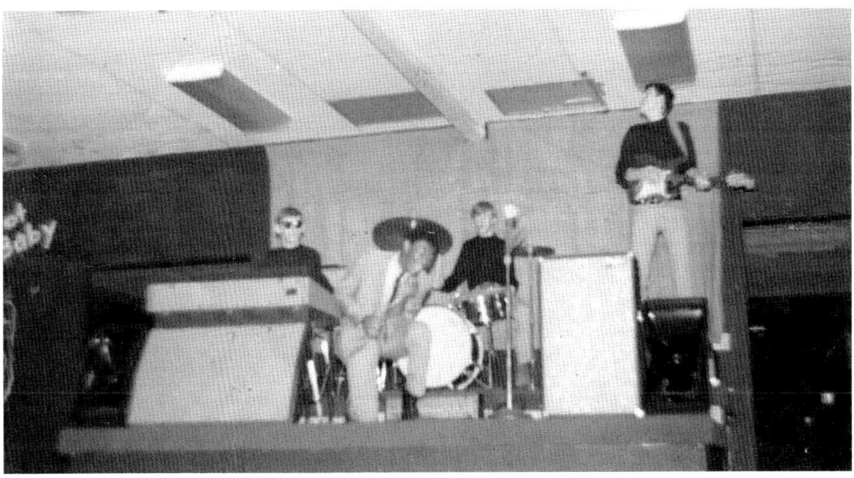

popular in the Top 40. If it was hot, we'd try to do it. We probably had about forty to fifty songs in our repertoire. I do remember being a little worried about playing at the Willowbrook Country Club by the swimming pool, but everything went fine there.

One place where I do remember being scared, although we weren't playing there, was a downtown club called the Snuff Dippers Ball that was across the street from the old post office above the Double Cola plant. Mike Byrom's dad owned some jukeboxes there, and I went with him to help change out the records. It was strictly a country music place with some tough-looking customers, and I got some bad looks; I was kind of nervous. They may have made some racist statements, but I don't remember. I tended to not let that stuff get to me, just let it roll off like water on a duck's back. You just had to do that sometimes.

I think being in the band made a difference in the way I handled the black-white thing. I remember going into the Sno-White on Whitesburg, where blacks had traditionally gotten their hamburgers around back. The band (including me) went in the front, and they served all of us without comment. There were a lot of places I would go into where blacks had not gone, at least up to that point. I kind of thought of myself as a "star" and expected to go into these places!

Really, we had a greater range of music than most of the other Huntsville bands. We got pretty popular. I remember girls would sometimes tear out a piece of their hair and throw it onstage.

Ivy Joe reflects on the other local musicians who inspired him:

We thought the Good Times were a really good group. When the Precious Few came along, they really challenged us; they were real talented and could do just about any kind of music. Howard Messer, Mike and Pat Couchois and Larry Byrom, who played trumpet, organ and guitar, made up the band. Larry's brother, Mike, played with us on bass and saxophone. That reminds me, Mike Byrom did a great version of "Yakety Sax" that was always a crowd pleaser, especially at the Peppermint Lounge.

As far as the most talented musicians around at the time, Larry Byrom without a doubt. As far as black musicians, Bo Dollar, who played organ and Ernest Jones's club, was real good. Willie Butler, whose nickname was "Spot," played a good guitar. He wrote "Self-Preservation," and Bill Brandon recorded it. Spot was a garbage collector in the daytime and played all around town at night. Of course Bill Brandon—we're cousins, by the way—was the most successful of all the black artists, having written and performed some hits, and playing with a number of big name artists. He spent some time in Canada and has a following in Europe. He's still got a great voice.

Left: W.C. Cowles (left) and Jimmy Gentry of the Precious Few. *Courtesy of W.C. Cowles.*

Below: Precious Few. *Courtesy of W.C. Cowles.*

Tommy Graham tells of the band's good fortune in attracting Chris Couchois as a drummer:

> *We were rehearsing one day and this little kid came over, little curly red-headed thirteen-year-old kid, and we were trying to do "Midnight Hour." It's got a little drum roll in the front, and our drummer just couldn't grasp it, and kid says, "Well, can I try?" and he sat down and just nailed it. That was Chris Couchois. From then on, he was our drummer.*

We hung out in Ivy's neighborhood a lot, and I just idolized Bo Dollar.

Well, of course like anybody does today takes the Leslie and turns it around to the ugly side, right? So you see the holes. You see the horns standing, not the pretty furniture side, because then the sound would blare louder, right? There's a horn in the top. Well actually two horns, one is a dummy, just for balance, but the sound only comes out of [one] *horn, so when it starts spinning it starts spinning or pulsing the sound. Well, the bottom has a big speaker facing down into this drum, and it has a scoop, so when that drum starts spinning with that scoop it makes the bottom speaker revolve around—you crank an organ with two switches. You hit the big swtch to get it going and then once it's up to speed then you turn that off and then you hit the next switch and that keeps it going so it spins that Leslie slowly and then it spins faster and faster and faster. Well, apparently, a momma rat had gone in the cabinet over the weekend and had a little litter of little tiny mice. There were probably eight or nine ladies sitting right there around me. All the sudden that thing starts spitting out these little rats—'bout cleared the place. Those poor women were up on the tables screaming. We laughed so hard. They were goin' "eeeek! eeek!" That was hilarious.*

They referred to me as a blue-eyed soul brother, and everybody kind of knew me. Me and Chris Couchois, we'd go down there all the time. Chris was only fifteen by now or something like that, you know. But after a while they started to let us play a couple of songs, all of us, and it was a real big hit, you know, it was unique.

Booker T was my mentor. I still play his music today. Ivy Joe and the Snowballs played at the University of Alabama in '66 or '67. Otis Redding was there, so it was before Otis Redding's day. Otis Redding, Sam and Dave and Booker T and the MGs. And Ivy Joe and the Snowballs! We started the show off. I met Booker T. Jones, kinda met him as we were setting up stuff. Well, he made fun of my organ. He goes, "What in the hell is that?" And I said, "That's an organ." And he said, "Fold that thing up, man, you're gonna play my B-3." And I memorized his draw bar settings. There's four sets of draw bars: two sets are for the top, two sets for the bottom, so you'll see the reverse keys on the left in black where there should be white. You can set one one way and the other another way, and quickly, right in the middle of the song, you can flip from one setting to the other. I memorized those draw bars, I mean I could sing 'em in my sleep, so that was a tremendous day.

Later on, Larry Byrom was impressed when he heard his little brother's band:

> *When I would come back from California while I was with Steppenwolf, I would see them. Mike said, "You have got to see this band." My brother was the bass player. I went to a rehearsal that was on Monte Sano mountain at a little house up at the end of that last road before Maple Hill Cemetery. I heard them rehearse, and I was blown away, because they were really good. And I thought it was a cool name, with the black-white thing, you know, the way they were mixed up. You have to remember, this was all still when being black was really kind of tough. But I don't remember ever hearing anybody say, "We don't want to mess with them because they've got a black singer," or anything like that. The prejudice was virtually nonexistent for Ivy Joe. He was one of the guys. He was an exception, really, one of the first.*

Ivy Joe Milan was not, as many people suppose, the first black student at Huntsville High School. That impression arises because his high-profile presence helped the process of integration in the school's community. Disregarding outdated racial divisions, Ivy Joe and the Snowballs bonded through rock and soul, and everybody danced.

Chapter 8
1967

Eight Miles High

Terry Barkley describes the peak of the Shandells' run as a band:

> *The high point of the Shandells, I think, was when we headlined the Madison County Fair music program. We played for a solid week. I remember heading over to the Coliseum after school and playing for four, five, six hours a night. The band got really tight, we had just the right personnel and we developed quite a following.*
>
> *I think it was 1967, because my brother was drafted in 1968. He decided to go into the navy thinking that he probably wouldn't have to serve in Vietnam if he was on a ship. Well, they did send him to Vietnam, and he served in a naval supply unit based at Chu Lai and was under fire almost every day! When he returned from his tour of duty, we got the Shandells back together for a short time. Eventually, three members of the group went to Vietnam, but not me. I ended up at Jacksonville State taking classes, playing in the Marching Southerners Drum Corps and also in several rock and roll bands after hours and on weekends. I eventually transferred to Florence State (now the University of North Alabama), where I served as a cadet officer in Advanced Army ROTC.*

Also in 1967, Billie Brown arrived in Huntsville and started playing guitar with Ivy Joe and the Snowballs:

My father retired from the army in March of 1967, and we moved back to Huntsville after being in El Paso for the last three years. A few months later, I stole his car and drove back to El Paso so I could graduate with my high school class. The superintendent of schools in El Paso was nice enough to meet with me then send me packing back to Alabama. I was attending Lee High School in Huntsville, but by the time I returned, I had been expelled. Oh well, another senior year, but this time at Huntsville High School.

It was the second year of integration at Huntsville High School. Councill High School, "the colored school," had been closed, and the situation was forced on all students. It was on everyone's mind, and there was a tinted atmosphere that I did not understand.

I had been raised in army school systems that had been integrated ever since I was in the first grade. I had lived in Japan, Puerto Rico and Panama, so I did not really know how everyone felt about school integration because it was quite a normal thing for me to attend school and socialize with an ethnically diverse student body. The general attitude at Huntsville High School was a parental- or societal-infused prejudice of the other race. But there was an intense curiosity of the "other" group because of the lifelong lack of social exposure to each other. The atmosphere was charged for something to happen. Hopefully it would be good.

I met Ivy Joe Milan and Tommy Graham in Mr. Von Tiesenhausen's class at Huntsville High School in September of 1967. They invited me to hear their band, Ivy Joe and the Snowballs, at the Epoch Teen Club at Five Points the following Sunday. There was a gathering of teenagers every Sunday afternoon there to hear the local bands play and hang out. Being a musician and new to Huntsville, I was very interested.

That Sunday, I went and immediately got involved with the Snowballs. Their drummer, Chris Couchois, was not there and needed a ride to the event. I volunteered my services, and Ivy, Tommy and I piled into the Cadillac I had borrowed from my dad, and so the story starts. Chris was impressed that he was being chauffeured to the event, and we started talking music. It was very simple; their guitar player, Eddie, was going off to college, and I was a guitar player. Put two and two together, and I was offered an audition.

The next Monday night, I went to the audition and started learning the songs that the Snowballs played. I was a British invasion and West Coast listener. I had no idea what "soul" music was, but the rhythms and chord patterns were familiar, and I had no trouble learning a few of the songs. About five songs and an hour later, they took a vote, and I became a Snowball. "Okay, you're in, pack up your gear. We are going over to the Peppermint Lounge to play." What? I only halfway know five songs and we are going to a club to perform? Well, that was the way it started and pretty much continued throughout those times and basically has never changed. We could do a gig together tonight.

I did not think it was peculiar or especially unique to play in a band with a black man. I had done so before in El Paso and other places. I was amazed at the popularity of Ivy Joe and the Snowballs. Was it the music or the integrated lineup? The music always seemed to get everyone on the dance floor, and that is the main thing you want to accomplish. This still happens today and every time we play, but more on that later. I guess the kids and adults we played for maybe saw the future, like Dr. King, or the music was just damn good.

I had to fake it a lot because I still did not know all of the songs. But my ineptitude was overcome by our showmanship, or I should say Ivy's showmanship. The girls made up for any lack of chord knowledge. I was damn sure going to learn all the songs so I could stay in the band. Sex or music, what was the motive to keep playing? I know, but should I tell?

So But So What play at a telethon. *Courtesy of Vannie Warren.*

The Sonics, with unknown guest singer. *Courtesy of Billie Brown.*

One afternoon, we loaded all of the equipment into a local private club and set up. We had a contract to play that evening. Later, when we arrived, Ivy was stopped at the door. "The man" said he could not come into the club. It was private and did not allow "his kind." So Ivy hung around outside while the rest of us collected the equipment. We didn't say anything to "the man," nor did we cause a disturbance. We just took it in stride that some places were not fully with the times and did not want to be integrated. So, we went up to Monte Sano and got drunk and got over it. I know it was a terrible thing for Ivy to experience. It did not happen often. But we all knew it could at any time. We all felt really bad about it, and there was nothing we could do about it.

Joe Hardin joined his first band in 1967:

For me, these guys were the big time—Ivy Joe, the Precious Few, the Tiks and the So But So What. They inspired me.

I joined my first rock and roll band in about 1967, and I played trumpet. We played "Walk Don't Run 65," "Watermelon Man," "Sleepwalk,"

"Spooky," etc. Two years later, in 1969, Abbey Road *came out, and I transitioned to guitar (the Beatles did not have a trumpet player, after all). Our goal was to play the second side of* Abbey Road *all the way through. We played almost exclusively Beatles songs, but we also played Traffic's "Low Spark of High Heel Boys," Hendrix's "Fire," "Jumpin' Jack Flash" and a few other Stones songs and Canned Heat's "Goin' Up the Country."*

We were not on the A circuit, so we primarily played "youth nights" at churches all over town and at pool parties. Our goal was to play at one of the armory shows, but we never made it. We played under the horrible names of Throckmorton Potsucker and the Stainless Steel Banana and the Steel Mind Cage. What were we thinking? Maybe that's why we didn't get the armory gig.

Big shows with local bands for me as an audience member were Ivy Joe and the Snowballs on stage at Whitesburg Junior High in probably '67 or '68, a sock hop. This was a big deal for us because we considered Ivy Joe to be the big time.

Ivy Joe was a real performer, just like the guys you saw on TV, I thought. I remember digging the fact that the band was integrated (at least I saw it that way) like Booker T. and the MGs. I saw the Precious Few and the Tics at several pool parties. My best friend at the time, Steve Hill (now a semi-famous evangelist), played a few gigs with the Precious Few on trumpet. I also remember seeing the So But So What at a Dunnavants fashion show. That was Danny and Vannie Warren—great band.

Another big moment for me in the sixties was Sam the Sham and the Pharaohs at the Madison County Coliseum probably in 1966 or 1967. That was my first up close and personal rock show, and it changed my life. I got to see how the professionals did it. My friend and I got backstage and got Sam's autographed picture. I wish I knew where that autographed picture was now. We also saw Paul Revere and the Raiders there sometime during the sixties. The Madison County Coliseum was a horrible venue, with incredibly bad sound.

Later on, the band called Felt, Mike Jackson and Stan Lee's band, was influential. These were my main local influences.

Where the Action Was

In the mid-1960s, traveling shows of national acts came to town. Segments of *Where the Action Is* were filmed in Big Spring Park, including one dance

Above: Ticket to Dick Clark's Happening '67. *Courtesy of Amy Chapin.*

Left: Rocker Keith Allison with policeman. *Courtesy of Dede Gilbert Horan.*

number filmed from above, in which the Action Dancers danced across Church Street and into Big Spring Park in a jazz routine choreographed to the Lovin' Spoonful's "Summer in the City."

The poster for a Dick Clark "Happening '67" sponsored by Jimmy Velvet promises all kinds of enticements: prizes like "His and Hers" motorcycles, a '67 Camaro that "stops traffic" with its "psychedelic light and sound show" and Irma, a "6 ft brunette who paints mod art with her hair to the music beat." The local band the Esquires would supplement the tour lineup, providing "Continuous Dancing." A "mod fashion show" would feature micro mini skirts and paper dresses. Jimmy Velvet would be on hand "singing all of his hits."

Proto-punk Dick Dodd of the Standells at the Coliseum. *Courtesy of Dede Gilbert Horan.*

Larry Byrom had an experience most rockers only dream of when he was "discovered" during a Dick Clark Caravan stop in Huntsville and invited to move to California to play on the rock and roll television show *Where the Action Is.*

> *The Precious Few played for the Dick Clark Caravan of Stars as the opening act. That's where I got spotted by Rudy Romero of the Hard Times and asked to come out to join them and play the* Where the Action Is *show. We were the opening act, and we all had paisley pants and matching shirts and we looked good. I had a conversation with Rudy Romero backstage, and he liked where I was coming from musically and I was a fairly good singer and I could play some really good guitar at that time. Within about*

Left: Elvis's friend Jimmy Velvet. *Courtesy of Dede Gilbert Horan.*

Below: Velvet Tone record. *Courtesy of Kip Shepherd.*

a week and a half, he called and said, "We've lost our bass player. Could you come out here and join us?" I was in the eleventh grade, and I talked to my dad about it. I said, "Dad, I'm gonna have to quit school. I need to get out there and do this because this could be my only shot." Dad always encouraged my music, so he said, "Go for it." So he gave me fifty bucks, and they sent me a plane ticket, and they picked me up in a limousine and they took me straight to a studio, Royal Pacific studio. So I went in the recording studio and picked that bass up and I played the fire out of that thing. And I recorded some vocals on that record by the Hard Times called Blew Mind, *played bass. Then back in the limo they took me to Laurel Canyon to this cool house where they had a little room set up for me.*

Larry Byrom had not been in California all that long when he became the guitarist for the band Steppenwolf. He explained that lead singer "John Kaye was the historian and wordsmith," but Byrom co-wrote the music for the albums *Monster* and *Steppenwolf 7*, albums that resonated with his friends

Phil "Fang" Volk, bassist for Paul Revere and the Raiders. *Courtesy of Dede Gilbert Horan.*

Larry Byrom, after he left Huntsville. *Courtesy of Larry Byrom.*

"Fang" and the band at the Coliseum. *Courtesy of Dede Gilbert Horan.*

back in Huntsville because the music was both demanding and engaging and the lyrics expressed themes that were relevant to their lives.

Most Huntsville musicians would find their California dreams deferred, but Larry's sister Gloria remembers the promise of those days:

> *The "feel" was absolutely electric in Huntsville back in the late sixties. The sound of the music was new to the world, and the message it brought was profound. We were a unique generation, and Huntsville held its own with all the powerhouse musicians from this area. The air was vibrant with excitement over possibilities we never imagined before. Music was our magic carpet ride.*

Years later, the Byrds songwriter Gene Clark told a Huntsville audience that he had written "Eight Miles High" when they were here on tour in the sixties.

Chapter 9

Hey, Mr. Spaceman

Ivy Joe and two of the Snowballs, Tommy Graham and Chris Couchois, were hanging out at the Nite Lite on Holmes Avenue when the news came that Martin Luther King Jr. had been assassinated in Memphis. For the Snowballs, club owner Ernest Jones was a hero that night:

> *Looking back on it, I guess I was most scared the evening we played at the Night Lite in April 1968 right after Dr. King had been killed. We were leaving the club, and the streets were packed with angry people, yelling and cursing. They began to scream at the Snowballs, just turned on them, basically for being white. People were just so frustrated and in grief. I intervened and tried to play the peacemaker, saying something like, "They didn't shoot him." Someone yelled out, "Well, we'll just get you too!" At that point Ernest Jones, the club owner, came out with a .38 revolver and said, "Break this up." He didn't allow anything to go on inside or outside his club; everyone knew he meant business, and the crowd backed off. We got out of there real fast in an old '56 Chevy that I had just bought.*

Tommy Graham's recollection varies slightly from Ivy Joe's, which is not unusual for an intense emotional memory:

> *We were sitting at a table in the Night Lite and I just remember somebody bustin' through the front door said, "The king is dead, the king is dead." And then you could just kinda hear a rumble around the room, and then*

> *everybody just stood up. And the look on their faces was scared. They all kinda turned around and looked at us. Well, Ernest Jones is behind the bar, he's the owner. He sees what's going on. And believe it or not, he pulls out a pistol and shot it through the ceiling, and everybody stopped, and he came over the bar, him and another bartender, and the band came down off the stage and they formed a circle around us. Ivy was part of the circle and me and Chris Couchois were encased in this little circle of black guys. He said, "We gotta get you outta here." And we just moved all together, through the crowd and through the front door.*
>
> *Now at this time the street had just filled up, it's packed almost like New Orleans on Mardi Gras. Just packed. Here we are in this little circle and we kinda pushed our way into the crowd. Well, the mob's moving, so we went with them up the street, to the square. I remember we got to the square, and the square was one way around, counterclockwise. And that's where the crowd went, and they marched around the square. From the west side we turned left, that would be the south side, and then we took off on a street to the right. We felt they saved our lives.*

Chris Couchois noticed that the assassination of Martin Luther King affected the camaraderie between black and white musicians because "our bonds with the black community had disintegrated." Musicians, with their commonly held language and culture, would reconnect, but it would take some time.

On the night Dr. King died, Val Ginter worked late at WAAY-TV and came home to find his neighbors terrified by their fears of what might happen next:

> *When Martin Luther King was killed, I was night director at WAAY-TV. We had just finished directing our evening news,* The WAAY of the World. *I was already married by then and living at 106 Grove Avenue, NW. When I got home after the late news, all these people were walking up and down Meridian and Grove carrying rifles. The lady who lived next door to me asked me, "Mr. Ginter. Don't you have a gun?" I just came home and went to bed. The next morning on our* Coffee Break *show, the host, Maury Farrell, commented on how beautifully the black community handled the situation with the marches down Meridian Street from Oakwood College and Alabama A&M. But the white people in my neighborhood around Pratt and Meridian were armed to the teeth the night before.*

Adrian Clift, a student at Butler High School ("Home of the Rebels"), recalls "a special assembly in the Butler Commons area when Martin Luther King was assassinated, I guess to try to calm things down."

Some musicians noticed that southern soul music seemed to more or less disappear, though that could have been a coincidence in a time of rapid change. Chris Couchois remembers the shift in the music: "We started playing rock music, no more soul. I can't think of the late sixties without thinking of a house we called the Shack. We would have jams that lasted for hours, stuff like Jeff Beck or Hendrix or Cream."

Joe Hardin started seeing connections he had not understood before, like the connection between prejudice against hippies and prejudice against people of other races:

> *Like many white people in the sixties in Alabama, I lived a kind of "double" existence as regards race. We were encouraged to consider ourselves better than blacks and to use racial epithets freely. Still, we had housekeepers who might as well have been members of the family. Very confusing for a kid. My mother, a very humane Christian woman, fought with these ambiguities all her life. Only people, both black and white, who grew up under the situation can appreciate the complexity of race relations in the South.*
>
> *I remember the moment when I realized what was going on. I must have been thirteen or fourteen. We were driving through a strip mall, and a boy with longish hair (for the time) was walking along. I thought he looked cool. My dad threw some kind of epithet at him, and I realized that I could not trust my dad's judgment about people, black people included. I started that very day trying to eradicate the racism and prejudice from my mind.*

Society was changing fast, at moments seeming to come unglued. Ivy Joe and the Snowballs had started their band in the exuberant energy of youthful optimism, with no expectation that the realities of life in the late 1960s would close in on them as quickly as they did. By the time Bobby Kennedy was assassinated in June 1968, Ivy Joe and the Snowballs had disbanded. Drummer Chris Couchois, the youngest Snowball, was still in high school.

Tommy Graham gives his perspective of the events that led to the band's reputation as "church thieves." While he had not heard the term "white privilege," Tommy recognized it when he saw it, because he got in less trouble than Ivy Joe:

In 1968, I got in trouble with the law for "borrowing" a microphone from the First Christian Church on Whitesburg Drive. My intentions were to return it that Saturday night after we played a gig at the Epoch Teen Club. Somehow that didn't work out, and we all got in trouble after Ivy was caught pawning it at Uncle Sam's pawnshop in downtown Huntsville. Fortunately, the pastor knew me and my parents and decided not to press charges. This was after my parents had taken me to his office and had me apologize. Which I did, sobbing in tears.

Ivy was not so fortunate. He went to court and was given the choice between jail time and joining the army. This was common practice at the time because the Vietnam War was raging and the military needed as many people as they could get, regardless of their moral standings. Ivy Joe was sent to Vietnam.

I was enjoying my good luck when just weeks later I received my draft notice in the mail. I was instructed to report to the armory in Montgomery, Alabama (all branches of service processed their inductees there), for my physical, which I did and returned home. A few weeks later, I received a letter from the army that I had failed my physical and was told to report back to the Montgomery armory to process out. I knew that I would fail that physical because two years earlier I was injured when I was riding with a friend when he wrecked his 1965 Mustang. I was in the passenger side and was thrown from the car, breaking my back in three places and cracking my skull. So I returned to Montgomery in high spirits, knowing that I had dodged the bullet and returned to process out of the army.

I was carrying my papers and was heading for the door to board the bus back to Huntsville in the parking lot when two marines in full dress uniform grabbed me and told me that I was required to take their physical. I explained to them that I had failed, but they said theirs was a little different. They never examined me and ran no tests. I was told to extend my index finger and then bend it, as if pulling a trigger. Since I could do that, I passed. So instead of boarding the bus back to Huntsville, I was on my way to boot camp at Parris Island, South Carolina. Back then, the marines weren't only "Looking for a few good men." They were also looking for some who would be expendable.

Parris Island

I endured nine weeks of intense physical training and even more intense mind conditioning, also known as brain washing, at Parris Island. I returned to Huntsville for two weeks' leave and looked up my old friends. I remember them telling me that I had changed. I had been reprogrammed and just didn't have control of my thoughts and actions. Thank you, marine training!

I was then transferred to Camp Lejeune, North Carolina. This is where I was trained for my "special" mission. Their intentions were to send a group of us undesirables across the DMZ, the De-Militarized Zone. This was a line that could not be legally crossed according to the Geneva Convention. We were supposed to inflict havoc on the North Vietnamese. We were to be flown by helicopter a hundred miles into enemy territory and make our way back on foot. We were told to enter small villages and find the papa san, the oldest man, and execute (that is, murder) him in front of the other villagers. This would instill fear in the folks and persuade them not to want to fight. Killing the papa san only was a modified plan. Originally, the mission would be to massacre the entire village. Apparently there had been some soldiers caught doing that, and it caused some really bad press. There was no way I was going to participate in this.

I went to my commanding officer and informed him that I was a conscientious objector. He just laughed and said that my category of marines didn't have the same privileges as real marines. I was to board a plane to Da Nang the next morning. That night, I dressed in civilian clothing, sneaked off base and hitchhiked my way back to Huntsville. A few months later, I was caught by the FBI. I arrived back to Camp Lejeune handcuffed with a three-month growth of hair. They took me to the barber and told him to only shave the top of my head. Then they escorted me all around the base, telling everyone that they had captured Bozo. Everybody got a big laugh out of that.

I stayed in jail there for several months and was given a military court-martial. An attorney was appointed to defend me. I told him that I just wanted out, but he would have nothing to do with that. I knew then that it was just a scam. My sentence was three months' jail time and then to return to active duty.

Canada

I could think of nothing else but escaping. I knew that when my three months were up that I would be on that plane to Da Nang. I worked the serving lines breakfast, lunch and dinner. A good friend of mine would come through the line every day, and he would always ask me how I was doing. We would have a few seconds to talk three times a day. He was the one that came up with the escape plan. The plan was for him to slip me a speed pill (amphetamine) and meet me outside of the compound fence that night with civilian clothing. I took the pill about two hours before they bedded us down. I was wired. I was in bed for about thirty minutes when I decided to make my getaway. My buddy was there and had the good sense to bring a couple of blankets to throw over the barbed wire. I scaled the fence, tore off my striped prisoner suit and put on the jeans and T-shirt that he had brought me, along with socks and tennis shoes. We got in his car, and he drove me to the interstate. I'll never forget him.

I made it back to Huntsville and hooked up with my girlfriend (my future wife), and we plotted our trip out of the country. Not wanting to risk getting caught, we slept in Three Caves in sleeping bags for a week. Then, with a twenty-dollar bill in my pocket, we set off and hitchhiked to New York City. We arrived in New York several days later broke and starving. It was freezing when we got there, and we didn't even have coats. We went to the Salvation Army, and they gave us warm coats and scarves. We hadn't eaten for days. Out of desperation, I saw a hippie sitting on the sidewalk, reading a comic book, and I decided to trust him and told him about my situation and that we needed help. I told him that I had deserted the marine corps, was running from the FBI and needed to get to Canada. He looked at me and said, "You need to go see the Quakers, man." He gave me directions to their meeting place in a basement down the street. When we arrived, they were in the middle of a meeting. The lady leading the folks in discussion looked up at us and said, "You're in trouble, aren't you? Are you hungry?" I said yes, we haven't eaten in days. She took us into the kitchen and fixed us sandwiches and milk. She told us that she could help us get to Canada and that we could stay with her and her husband.

Tommy and Linda Graham spent five years in Canada before President Gerald Ford offered amnesty to draft dodgers. They flew to Indiana, and at Fort Benjamin Harrison, Tommy Graham, keyboard player and founder of Ivy Joe and the Snowballs, was officially discharged from the military.

Chapter 10

Moon, Turn the Tides

No one can say for sure when one era gives way to the next. Did the sixties end with the assassinations of Martin Luther King Jr. and Bobby Kennedy? Or with NASA's successful lunar landing in July 1969? For trombonist Tom Winstead Sr., the lunar landing meant he could finally stop working eighty hours a week and start playing with the Charlie Lyle Orchestra. For his son, bassist Tom Winstead Jr., the cultural shift from the sixties to the seventies occurred "when Cream and the Beatles broke up, and bands like Jethro Tull and Mott the Hoople came out of England. That would be the break point." Times were changing, and music was changing with the times.

For Ivy Joe Milan, things took a drastic turn when his troubles landed him in Vietnam.

> *As I've said, by early '68 I was getting into a lot of trouble. Actually, I had already volunteered to go into the army, but when I got into trouble, it nullified my military commitment. Earl Cloud was my attorney, and he was on a Draft Board down around Cullman. He signed some papers and told me to go down to the Montgomery draft office and wait there until they called my name. Eventually they did, I got into the army for two years and left Huntsville kind of on the run. When I came back to Huntsville on leave, the police picked me up for questioning, but since I was in the army and due to go to Vietnam, they just let it roll on. I was in Vietnam during '68 and '69.*

To Terry Barkley, there were a number of reasons why a band might not make it:

> *A lot of local bands started up in the sixties. I see it as a wave triggered by the Beatles and the British Invasion, but only a few lasted more than a few months to a year. People lost interest, graduated, moved away, got married, whatever, and bands usually broke apart pretty quickly. It was fun but grueling. The old saying that you've really got to* love *it to keep doing it applies here; there certainly wasn't any money in it. What (very) little money that came in from gigs usually got plowed back into new instruments and equipment. It was also incredibly time-consuming. You might play a two-hour gig, but with setup, breakdown and travel, you'd spend eight to nine hours on it and maybe, maybe, get forty dollars per person. There'd be long droughts where you couldn't get a gig, followed by an exhausting period of playing. No wonder most groups didn't survive for long! Also, there were the personality clashes within the band itself, plus everyone wanting to go musically in different directions.*

George Vail said the Xiles were the first hippie group in Huntsville, but the band called the In was also headed in the hippie direction:

> *The In played almost all cover songs. The Byrds, Turtles and Lovin Spoonful, plus the Beatles and the rest of the top acts of those years, Young Rascals and the black soul players like Wilson Pickett. Then original music mostly with the Xiles, but some covers too, of Ray Davies and the Kinks mostly and some blues music too. The Xiles were the first band in town to be independent, and it kept us out of the inner circles of Huntsville mainstream musicians. We were the first hippie group of Huntsville. The conservative kids hated us. Then, on January 30, 1969, I was inducted into the U.S. Army.*

For the In's Bill Peck, the band's repertoire suited his musical taste:

> *Eddie Burton and I started playing together as a duo singing stuff like Peter and Gordon, and Chad and Jeremy. Gradually, George Vail and Fred Sanders joined us in the Wessex Combo, which was the early In. We changed our original format from a folk-based duo to a commercial rock band. We became the In, and Bobby Land joined us on keyboards, some guitar and vocals. We worked constantly on three- and four-part harmonies. We recorded in Memphis and Nashville.*

The sixties slid right into the seventies for me. They didn't cause any drastic changes in my music, but the lifestyle I lived resulted in a lot of little ones. If anything, my music expanded to relate to the troubles the everyday person has to deal with.

Drummer Greg King had lived in Huntsville as a small child, where he attended Farley Elementary during the segregated days. He looks back to the early sixties and remembers classmates much too old to be in his grade because Farley would let students out of school to do farm work. When Greg returned to Huntsville for his last year of high school, a lot had changed. He had developed skills that showed he was a drummer to be taken seriously, and Huntsville's music community welcomed him, apparently overlooking the fact that he was too young to be playing in a bar's house band:

Huntsville's a pretty place, and I've watched it grow because I've been here off and on. My dad was in the military, and for '66, '67 and '68 we were in Germany, and that's when I got into drum playing. I met this white guy there named Regis, and he was playing in a band. Remember that song "Tighten Up"? Well, Archie Bell was drafted in the service, and he lived in the same military housing that we did. I was really into the Rascals, Jimi Hendrix, Buddy Miles and Santana. I called it acid rock.

The white guy I met in Germany, Regis, helped me build a drum set piece by piece. There were always leftover pieces, like a bass drum that had a cardboard box because it didn't have a head on it. And one of my stands was one of those ashtrays on a stand with a tent pole in it, and he gave me a cymbal and a high hat. I learned by ear, with records. Basically, I really liked jazz, because I learned so many rudiments. I could watch what Regis did and just turn around and do it. It was a gift. I was very fortunate.

Came back and went to Lee for senior year. When I was back here, I was about eighteen, and my dad bought me a set of drums. I started playing at the VFW. I wasn't old enough to be in there. No one said anything about it. It didn't matter. At the VFW on Stokes Street, there was one way in and one way out. It opened up at nine in the morning and closed at two in the morning, and people were there all day. It was centered in the area of all the projects, so everybody could get to it. It was not big, everybody was jammed in, but everybody had a good time. It was a young age group. I played with Curtis and Charles Marshall at the VFW. Every musician in town played at the VFW one time or another. There was a house band, but people would come sit in.

THE COTTON CLUB

When Bill Brandon asked Greg King to be his drummer, Greg began to think of himself as a real professional. Greg remembers the Cotton Club, with its house band the Royal Company, as Huntsville's most racially integrated rock and roll scene. Bill Brandon held high standards for the band: no drinks on the stage, be punctual, attend rehearsals every workday. Each band member was expected to both play and sing. According to Brandon, there were perhaps five hundred songs in the Royal Company's repertoire, including at least one song from every major group on the radio. Greg King remembers:

> *I was playing with Curtis Marshall, Bruce Bennett and Spot* [Willie Butler] *at a little center by where Butler Terrace used to be. Well, Bill Brandon shows up in a green Cadillac with a white top, with this white guy Sweet Pea, Carl, they pull up and he says, "Man, I need a drummer." I said, "Really?" And he said, "Yeah, I really need a drummer."*

Bill Brandon and the Royal Company at Big Spring. *Left to right*: Tim Spivey, Kurt Schweigart, Lorraine Johnson, Doug Shaw, Dee Clark, Bill Brandon, Carl Edwards and Greg King. *Courtesy of Bill Brandon.*

That's when I started playing with him, and it took off from there. I went to the school of Bill Brandon. We were like celebrities. People asking for your autograph. And it was mixed, too. The band was mixed and the crowd was mixed. There were no other places like that. The Cotton Club was unified because it was balanced. We were working six or seven nights a week.

Then I had a tragedy at the Cotton Club. We all did. I lost close to $3,000 worth of drums when someone set the club on fire. I had just made my last payment on 'em, and I was gonna have 'em insured on Monday. When we got through that Sunday, I hadn't been home for forty-five minutes when my roommate came in and said, "The club's on fire." And I went down there and saw. I had the fiberglass, blue clear. It was hard to start over. See, our band was so hot back then, people were coming from miles around to go to the Cotton Club. That same night, the Diplomat also burned down. Same night. A lot of musicians lost equipment that night. Danny Wilder lost his keyboards. It was the end of an era.

Bill Brandon is proud of the deep pool of talent and high level of musicianship in Huntsville.

Yeah, I'm telling you we used to always boast about the talent here 'cause a lot of people come here from out of town, bands you know and entertainment, and they would get up and play and do this and that and they'd be hollering for the crowd to clap, and saying, "Aw, y'all ain't into

The futuristic-themed Parkway Country Club, later the Plush Horse. *Courtesy of William Hampton, Huntsville Revisited.*

> *it." Well, man, you can't come here with that attitude. You gotta come here and really play, because people in Huntsville are used to seeing good entertainment. You can't come here and try to snow 'em. You've got to work.*
>
> *You know Walter Clyde Orange, with the Commodores, played drums for us for a while. He sang "Brick House." And one of the regular Temptations, Artie Wilson, he's from here. Tina Turner used to eat breakfast at Sambo's when she played the Plush Horse. Good entertainment has been here for a loooong time. You go back to Wilson Pickett, Ray Charles, B.B. King—and Little Milton, we played together for years.*
>
> *I listen to country now because I love music. I love the lyric, I love the expression, I love the story, I love the expertise that the musicians show. I mean, they're saying a lot more than what's going on now.*
>
> *Today's blues ain't about nothin' as far as I am concerned, they're so watered down. These kids have no idea. Now, that might just be an old man talking. But I'll tell you one man around here who can slap it down on you, and I'm talking about Microwave Dave. He understands. He understands soul. There's a lot of talent here, a lot of good musicians. Huntsville is the watering hole.*

Huntsville's wellspring includes a community full of musicians who "can slap it down on you." Huntsville musicians will continue to reach across generational and racial lines to jam and learn from one another because they know they share a common language of rhythm and harmony. As Greg King explains, "To musicians, everybody else is like civilians."

Bibliography

Cashin, Sheryll. *The Agitator's Daughter.* New York: Public Affairs, 2008.

Cooley, Billy Joe. "Grady Reeves, the Promoter." *Old Huntsville Magazine* 220 (June 2011).

Dupre, Daniel S. *Transforming the Cotton Frontier.* Baton Rouge: Louisiana State University Press, 1997.

Gaillard, Frye. *With Music and Justice for All: Some Southerners and Their Passions.* Nashville, TN: Vanderbilt University Press, 2008.

Guralnik, Peter. *Sweet Soul Music: Rhythm and Blues and the Southern Dream of Freedom.* New York: HarperCollins, 1986.

Halberstam, David. *The Fifties.* New York: Fawcett-Columbine, 1993.

Hereford, Sonnie, III. *A Civil Rights Journey.* DVD. Decatur, AL: Calhoun Community College, 1999.

Hereford, Sonnie Wellington, III, and Jack D. Ellis. *Beside the Troubled Waters.* Tuscaloosa: University of Alabama Press, 2011.

Pollock, Dan. *Blues for the White Boy*. Unpublished manuscript with chapters available on the web at home.hiwaay.net/~dizzy/pages/DPollack.htm.

Robertson, David. *W.C. Handy: The Life and Times of the Man Who Made the Blues.* New York: Alfred A. Knopf, 2009.

Rohr, Nancy. *Echoes of the Past: Old Mahogany Table Stories.* Huntsville, AL: Silver Threads Publishing, 2010.

Szwed, John F. *Space Is the Place: The Lives and Times of Sun Ra.* New York: Pantheon, 1997.

Towery, Tommy. *The Baby Boomer's Guide to Growing Up in the Rocket City.* Huntsville, AL: Tommy Towery, 2010.

Wesley, Fred. *Hit Me Fred: Recollections of a Sideman.* Durham, NC: Duke University Press, 2002.

White, Charles. *The Life and Times of Little Richard.* Cambridge, MA: Da Capo Press, 1994.

Index

L

M

O

P

R

S

T

V

W

Z

About the Author

Jane DeNeefe, coauthor of *Alabama's Civil Rights Trail: An Illustrated Guide to the Cradle of Freedom*, lives in Huntsville, Alabama. A former bookseller and community columnist for the *Huntsville Times*, she has contributed to the WLRH public radio program *Writer's Corner*, the web magazine *Swampland: Cultures of the South*, *Encyclopedia of Alabama* and other publications. DeNeefe earned a BA in history from the University of Alabama in Huntsville.

Courtesy of Doug Bennett.